Canoe Camping Vermont & New Hampshire Rivers

Canoe Camping
Vermont &
New Hampshire Rivers

A guide to 600 miles of rivers for a day,
weekend, or week of canoeing

SECOND EDITION

Roioli Schweiker

Backcountry Publications   Woodstock, Vermont

An invitation to the reader...

Rivers are notorious for changing course. Dams wash out, storms
and floods rearrange rocks, and new bridges and roads alter access
points. If you run these rivers and find they have changed since this
edition went to press, the author and publisher would appreciate
hearing your corrections for future editions. And if you have
suggestions for other rivers—or new books—we would like to hear
those, too. Address all correspondence:

Editor, Canoe Camping
Backcountry Publications
P.O. Box 175
Woodstock, VT 05091

Library of Congress Cataloging in Publication Data

Schweiker, Roioli.
  Canoe camping, Vermont & New Hampshire rivers.

  1. Canoes and canoeing—Vermont—Guide-books.
2. Camping—Vermont—Guide-books. 3. Rivers—Vermont—
Recreational use. 4. Canoes and canoeing—New Hampshire—
Guide-books. 5. Camping—New Hampshire—Guide-books.
6. Rivers—New Hampshire—Recreational use. I. Title.
II. Title: Canoe camping, Vermont and New Hampshire
rivers.
GV776.V5S38   1985   917.43′0443   85-3870
ISBN 0-942440-22-6

© 1977, 1985, 1989 by Roioli Schweiker
Second edition: third printing, 1990

Published by Backcountry Publications, Inc.
A Division of The Countryman Press, Inc.
Woodstock, Vermont 05091

Text and cover design by Richard Widhu

ACKNOWLEDGMENTS

In appreciation to all those who helped make this book possible:

The people who allowed me to load canoes, park or camp on their property; the Northern Vermont Canoe Cruisers, Normand Lavoie, Dick Trudell, Doug Laiho, and Bruce Hodgeman for information on the Lamoille and Winooski Rivers; Herman Peakey for historical notes on the Missisquoi.

In addition to many of the persons listed below, Ray Gonda, Greg Smith, Ian Spencer, Al Roberts and Al Stairt helped check rivers for the revised edition.

Judy Butterfield Roberts, for photographic assistance; Clark Curtis and Walter Banfield, who taught me to canoe; my companions on these rivers, Alexander Murphy, Rachel Walker, Jane Jackson, Holly Anderson, Ralph Tyrrell, Lawrence K. Reilly, Peter Reilly, Lucie Strayer, Alden Rodgers, Dorothy Wilson, and Brian Pierce; and my husband, Robert; my son, Roy; my daugther, Viloya; and Boukey.

Roioli Schweiker

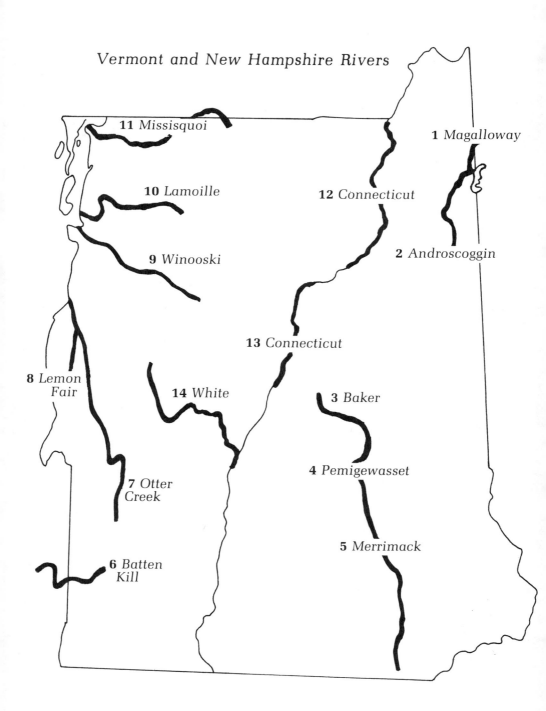

Vermont and New Hampshire Rivers

11 Missisquoi

1 Magalloway

10 Lamoille

12 Connecticut

9 Winooski

2 Androscoggin

13 Connecticut

8 Lemon
Fair

14 White

3 Baker

4 Pemigewasset

7 Otter
Creek

5 Merrimack

6 Batten
Kill

Contents

INTRODUCTION

COMMENTS ON THE SECOND EDITION

Reflecting upon the observations I had made while checking rivers for this revision, I was struck by three things:

The rivers themselves have changed very little; in a few cases a new channel has cut through a narrow neck, or occasionally a van-sized rock or two has rolled over to alter the make-up of a single rapid. However, the power of the river has greatly affected the works of man associated with it. Three large dams and one small one have gone out, to the temporary benefit of canoeists. Bridges have been damaged, and in some cases replaced.

The relationship of man to the river has also changed. The rivers are much cleaner then they were. In most cases the words "smelly" and "unattractive" could be deleted from the descriptions. Parks are being opened along the river and "greenways" figure in city planning.

The number of canoeists has greatly increased, and rafts and tubes are often seen on the rivers. Those who seek solitude on the rivers have to look harder now. Others appreciate the proliferation of canoe liveries with shuttle service. A few new campgrounds have opened. However, their number has been more than offset by the loss of many more pleasant sites where canoeists are no longer welcome to camp, due to overuse and lack of consideration for the landowner, your host. Be thoughtful — don't be the cause of additions to this list!

Comments and corrections are requested. However, the rest of you remember that even if I am aware of a change it will not magically alter the text of books already printed! Canoe under control at all times.

Many of you have recognized me along the river, and I look forward to seeing many more of you there in the future.

GENERAL INFORMATION

The canoe trips described here introduce you to some lesser-known Vermont and New Hampshire rivers as well as a few more popular runs. A chief attraction of these rivers is their accessibility. All are convenient to numbered highways, making arrival and car shuttling relatively simple, and numerous bridges and launching spots offer a fair degree of flexibility. The many access points allow you to run these rivers as a series of day trips or short camping trips, and none has quotas or requires advance registration. You need only obtain permission to cross or use privately owned property.

The river trips are arranged by watershed and run from just under 20 miles to over 80 miles. All offer a weekend or more of leisurely family canoeing and generally have enough water to be run for some of their length throughout the usual canoe camping season (mid-May to early autumn).

No trip is extremely demanding, but the descriptions assume basic canoeing knowledge and some experience in selecting rivers and landing spots above ledges and dams. Those less skilled should use caution and inspect all trouble spots in advance from the shore. This guide does not explain how to canoe; it does describe places to canoe and tells what to expect from each river.

In other respects, these river differ considerably. Some flow through sparsely settled woodlands, others across rolling farmland, and a few through cities. Some are entirely flatwater; others have rapids of varying length and difficulty. Two consist almost entirely of rapids. Although only a few big rapids have heavy water during the summer, experienced canoeists should find the lower water on these trips as challenging in its own way as roaring rapids. While warmer water and weather reduce danger, shallow water calls for greater skill in reading water and maneuvering a canoe.

Along with river descriptions, I have also included directions for short hikes near the river banks and notes on swimming holes, campsites, picnic areas, and historical sites which should help you choose a river suited to your particular interests.

SAFETY

No guidebook can substitute for canoeing skill and alertness. If you cannot stop in the distance you can see ahead, you are canoeing beyond your ability. It is possible to stop anywhere within a canoe length or two—even in the middle of a rapid—if you know how.

Novice paddlers should consult books that explain techniques of setting (bow downstream) and ferrying (bow upstream) directly across a fast current among rocks so that you do not lose ground. Always make practice runs on familiar rivers, preferably with a group that has rescue potential.

Keep your canoe under control. When landing in a fast current, your upstream end should always touch in to shore first. Approach sharp river bends cautiously on the inside, again with the stern well in toward shore for easy landing in case any obstacles, such as fallen trees, should suddenly appear.

Federal laws require a "personal flotation device" for each person on board. Serious canoeists wear a comfortable life jacket whenever running rapids, canoeing lakes in a wind, or wearing encumbering clothing (rainsuits, rubber boots). Poor swimmers should always wear life jackets, and nonswimmers should not canoe on rivers at all.

HAZARDS

Next to PWI (paddling while intoxicated), the chief cause of serious canoeing accidents is getting entangled in fallen trees. Their location cannot be documented, as conditions may change overnight. They are usually located around blind corners where the current sweeps the canoe into them and are especially hazardous in high water.

While trees may produce the same sort of hydraulics as rocks or other obstacles, they are also likely to have water flowing UNDER them, with submerged branches that prevent free passage of objects.

Picture the following scenario: the trunk of the tree is just above water level. A canoe strikes it and swings broadside. The current sucks the upstream gunwale under, and the paddlers wash under the boat, where tree branches keep them from surfacing.

The only protection is to canoe conservatively and under control at all times.

Dams, as well as PWI, are a particular hazard. The current often speeds up just before them, and retaining walls or steep banks may also confine the river. Dam gates open and close in seemingly arbitrary fashion, and the water level in the river below may quickly rise or fall as much as several feet. Most people recognize the dangers in a high dam or steep drop, but the backroller of a fairly low dam or ledge can sometimes trap a canoe—and canoeist—where they may churn around in the froth indefinitely.

Black flies are usually at their peak for a couple of weeks during June, while mosquitoes are active throughout the summer. Defenses against insects range from wearing a headnet and gloves along with clothing which has zippers and elastic instead of buttons, to applying a wide selection of sprays and ointments, or to simply staying home during the worst of the bug season. In summer camping, a bug-proof tent is a must for all but the most repellent old woodsman.

Learn to recognize and avoid poison ivy; unfortunately, this plant favors sunny river banks. The new oral poison ivy preventative minimizes the problem for those who are especially susceptible.

A tan you may have already acquired is no protection against a full day of exposure to powerful rays of sun reflecting off the water. Reflected sunlight can burn you even on cloudy days, so take cover-up clothing and sun hats, and put them on before it's too late. More summer trips are spoiled by an overdose of sun than by anything else. Sunglasses reduce glare reflected off the water.

Roof and 3 sides give latrine privacy and rain protection. Can on right holds paper. Seat folds.

CLOTHING

Many people like to canoe in a bathing suit; this is fine for a while, but be sure to take along more protective clothing—a hat, a long-sleeved shirt, pants or a full skirt, socks, and gloves.

Snowfalls as late as May are not uncommon, and even summers are often cold enough to warrant paddling in wool slacks and shirts. Carry a spare set of woolen clothing in case of an accident or a sudden drop in temperature. Extra woolens frequently make the difference between continuing a trip and going home. Blue jeans and sweat shirts are the worst possible choice for canoeing; they hold water like a sponge, are chilly when wet, and take forever to dry.

Wading shoes should be worn, particularly on rivers with rapids. Sneakers are usually sufficient, but someone lining or wrestling with a loaded canoe in shallow rapids might prefer more protection.

A rainsuit is the best protection the canoeist has against the weather. The plastic ones usually do not last even one trip; while the nylon ones are more expensive, their durability makes the difference worthwhile. Ponchos dangerously hamper your swimming ability and also get in the way of paddling.

EQUIPMENT

The equipment you choose for a canoe camping trip should reflect your own taste and budget along with the type of trip planned. Basic gear includes a canoe, paddles, lines, waterproof packs, and an emergency kit. If you need more information on canoe camping gear, consult books on the subject or talk with experienced canoeists and reputable canoe outfitters. Beginners can find several canoe outfitters in northern New England who rent all the equipment necessary for a comfortable trip. Names of rental outfitters can be obtained from local chambers of commerce, advertisements in canoeing magazines, or the yellow pages.

While almost any type of canoe will do for canoe camping, one 15 to 17 feet long is best for these rivers. Canoes of this length are large enough to carry a reasonable load yet are easy to handle and portage. Touring kayaks are popular in some areas.

A third paddle provides a spare for emergencies and is handy if you use paddles of different length for smooth water and for rapids. Since I am small, I need the powerful leverage of a 6-foot paddle to slam the stern of a loaded canoe sideways in a rapid, but I use a shorter one to paddle in quieter water.

Attach a 20-foot, painter (rope), 3/8 inch in diameter, to each end of your canoe. These lines are useful for tying up, lining past rapids, hauling up steep banks, and if worst comes to worst, they are a great help in rescuing a swamped canoe. Nylon resists abraision, but some people like the plastic lines that float. Smaller lines may be strong enough but they are hard to grip with a cold, wet hand and tend to kink up and knot.

Waterproofing essential equipment is a bit of a nuisance but worth the effort. All kinds of waterproof packs are available at sporting goods stores, but some advertised as water**proof** are only water **repellent**. **TEST** in advance. Most of them work well when new, but many become less effective as they get older. Before purchasing any waterproof pack, consider how easy it is to open and close, to portage, and to tie into a canoe. If you can find them, old army ammunition boxes come in a variety of sizes and make excellent waterproof packing for small items and cameras. So do the large institution-size plastic jars for foods like pickles and mayonnaise. You might try to obtain some of these from your neighborhood restaurant or school lunch program. Friction tops tend to pop off under stress, so use screw-top containers. Sometimes you need an extra liner in the lid to make the container waterproof; one can be cut from a cardboard food package. Plastic garbage bags are too flimsy to offer useful protection.

Waterproof bags for packing clothing, bedding, and foodstuffs are easy and inexpensive to make from waterproof cloth, waterproof glue, a 24-inch shoelace, and some thread. Use **waterproof** not water-repellent cloth; nylon coated with rubber or plastic is best. Cut the material into a rectangle twice the size of the finished bag (45 by 32 inches works nicely), and hem one long edge. Apply waterproof glue to one short edge and half the unhemmed long edge (check your glue to assure its effectiveness on your material), fold the cloth over so that the hemmed edge forms an opening, weight it, and allow the glue to dry. Machine stitch through the glue around the outside edges, and stitch the shoelace to the outside of the bag, 1 inch from the top.

To close the bag properly, do not pack it more than two-thirds full. Tie the string tightly around the top, press out the air, and fold the top over. Then tie the ends of the string around both the flap and the flattened bag. To protect the waterproof bag from punctures or wear, place it inside a cloth bag.

On a serious white water trip, I pack my equipment in a strong plastic bag placed in two waterproof bags and then in a water-repellent Duluth pack or duffle bag. Protected in this manner, my equipment has remained completely dry through a solid week of rain and two upsets.

All your equipment, except possibly a rock collection or a sack of canned goods which can be jettisoned, should be tied into the canoe so it will not slide around or be lost in a spill. The school of thought which suggests not tying in your gear has little to recommend it. Should you swamp or capsize, only a very efficient rescue squad could salvage loose gear before it floated off. Furthermore, a properly waterproofed duffle bag floats high in the water and tied in a swamped canoe will improve the canoe's balance and increase its buoyancy. To tie in your gear, use a light rope which can be cut easily should the canoe be pinned.

Your small packet of emergency items should include a first aid kit and a roll of duct tape. The tape is indispensible for patching holes in canoes, rainsuits, and other items. If applied to a dry surface, it continues to hold after it gets wet. A small sewing kit, complete with thread, needles, pins, buttons, extra cloth, and folding scissors is very handy. Also take along a knife, a small tube of waterproof glue, extra cord, waterproof matches, and a compass.

Fold-over tie method for sealing a soft waterproof bag.

CANOEING WITH CHILDREN

Properly introduced to it, children enjoy a canoe camping trip as much as adults. My own children began canoeing at a young age and are still canoeing.

Children should not canoe camp on rivers with white water until age eleven or twelve, or when old enough to swim with confidence. Children must have confidence that they can stay afloat and get to shore under various conditions. Children should learn to swim in fast water and waves—it is essential practice for a spill in the rapids. Another way to maintain interest is to get children their own equipment. Young children find regular paddles, especially those for white water, too cumbersome to manage. My daughter had her own red paddle with a special design and her name on it, to which she still has a sentimental attachment. Do not force your children to paddle. Children should also have their own properly-fitting life jacket and rain gear.

On flatwater trips, you might bring nature books to help identify wildlife and geologic structures. Plan time for children to explore the woods, swim, or fish.

CAMPING

Private campgrounds, some catering to canoeists, front a few of these rivers and are mentioned in the text. I have not attempted to name each one separately, since campgrounds, like rental outfitters, come and go. Current listings of all New Hampshire and Vermont campgrounds are available from government agencies in each state. Local chambers of commerce also offer lists of campgrounds in their area.

Many of these rivers, however, have few or no campgrounds along their banks, so you must make your own arrangments in advance with individual property owners. Most flow through farmland for some of their distance, and if approached properly, many farmers do allow canoeists to camp on their property. If permission to camp is refused, be courteous and understanding, and leave; if it is granted, be considerate, quiet, and unobstrusive. Take your litter and trash with you, and if you have permission for a fire, be careful and don't leave messy, charred remains. Remember that farmers depend on their fields and pastures for their livelihood—leave gates as you find them and walk along the fence lines rather than across the fields. The granting of permission to canoeists who follow you is determined by your behavior.

Some new campsites have been opened along the rivers, but many more have been closed by owners withdrawing permission to camp in areas which we formerly used.

TUBING

The use of innertubes, air mattresses and other floating objects has had a great upsurge in popularity. They have the advantage of being cheap, portable and available, and some places even rent them. Tubing is fun, but it is also dangerous. Tubers have little visibility ahead, and (like many canoeists) don't know the proper way to control their craft. Many have drowned by being swept under trees or over falls. Note that many people canoeing on these same stretches of river will be wearing lifejackets!

Beginners at tubing should select a stretch of river which is known either from other people or visual inspection to be free of hazards. Select a sunny day with the temperature well above 70°. Plan on a maximum of an hour floating, and allow for time to get out of the water and warm up along the way. Mountain streams are still very cold even in the summer.

Turtles sun themselves on logs.

We often carry tubes on our canoe trips, and at an interesting stretch of rapids instead of carrying the canoe back and rerunning it, we carry the tubes back instead. The tubes give the canoes extra flotation in the rapids, and make "beanbag" chairs around camp.

HIKING

Several hiking trails adjoin these rivers. The Long Trail, Vermont's Green Mountain footpath, crosses the Winooski and the Lamoille along the portions described here, and the Appalachian Trail crosses the White River at West Hartford. Directions for short hikes along these and other paths and roads which lead to particularly interesting summits, gorges, or ponds are given in the individual river sections.

ADDRESSES

Current listings of campgrounds (in New Hampshire, called "New Hampshire Camping Guide") and excellent state highway maps (which also list historical sites and state parks) are available from:

Division of Economic Development
P.O. Box 856
Concord, New Hampshire 03301
or
Vermont Information/Travel Division
Agency of Development and Community Affairs
Montpelier, Vermont 05602

For information regarding fishing conditions and regulations, contact the following:

New Hampshire Fish and Game Department
34 Bridge Street
Concord, New Hampshire 03301
or
Vermont Fish and Wildlife Department
Agency of Environmental Conservation
Montpelier, Vermont 05602

For information on Vermont's Long Trail, write:
Long Trail Guide
c/o Green Mountain Club
Box 889
Montpelier, Vermont 05602

The Appalachian Mountain Club promotes canoeing and hiking throughout New England; lists of local canoe chapters and other information can be obtained from:
Appalachian Mountain Club
5 Joy Street
Boston, Massachusetts 02108

USING THE RIVER DESCRIPTIONS

Each canoe trip includes maps, a brief introduction to the river, a summary table, and detailed descriptions for each river segment.

The maps in this book are intended for use in conjunction with a good highway map as well as USGS topographic sheets. The approximate scale is the same for all the maps and is 1 inch to 3 miles. The following symbols are standard:

river ~~~~~~   railroad ++++++++++++

road ▬▬▬▬   path - - - - - - -

launching ramp □   covered bridge ⌂

A good highway map should get you to your starting point and provide a general picture of the river's course and the terrain through which it flows. You can get these maps from state tourist bureaus or from gasoline stations.

The maps that accompany the descriptions were drawn specifically for this guidebook and show the break points, hazardous obstructions, difficult rapids, bridges, nearby roads, and hiking trails mentioned in the text. The trip runs from the top of the map to the bottom.

Each river has been broken down into short sections. Where feasible, each segment contains water conditions of similar difficulty. In some instances, break points occur at the most likely spot to end or begin a trip (such as dams). In many cases, these segments also make good day trips, but they were not specifically chosen for that reason.

"Right bank" and "left bank" as used in the text always refer to your position as if you are in the river facing downstream, regardless of your actual orientation.

I have not attempted to give a foot-by-foot description of each river. Rather, this guide should provide a general description of the type of canoeing you can expect on each river as well as the locations of all more difficult spots. Note: rivers often change abruptly, so use caution, and always have your canoe under control.

Meaningful estimates cannot be given for the time needed to cover the rivers. Everybody paddles at a different rate, current speed changes with different water levels, and the wind may either be with you or against you. Furthermore, people stop at different times to watch birds, pick flowers and berries, examine rocks, swim, fish, take photographs, hike, and recover from accidents. In general, it takes a large group longer to cover a given distance than a small one.

Remember to leave time for necessary car shuttles. This can be a big time waster, particularly if it is poorly organized. Good logistics can greatly increase the time you have available for canoeing.

I have also not attempted to rate the scenery. Some people want nothing but wilderness, while others prefer their riverbanks studded with white church steeples and old mills. Civil engineers like bridges, and gardening enthusiasts inspect the crops.

SUMMARY TABLES

Each river trip is accompanied by a summary chart: cumulative mileages to the left of the break points refer to the total distance from the start to the break points; the ratings and special difficulties noted on the right refer to those sections of the river that run between two break points.

Mileages. The mileages given in the chart and in each river description were usually measured from the 15-minute USGS topographic maps to the nearest ¼ mile. Cumulative distances were measured from an arbitrary starting point and cover the entire river segment, including parts which must be portaged. These figures also appear in parenthesis throughout the text as reference points.

River Rating. Throughout this book, I have used the international white water rating scale to describe the relative difficulty of each stretch of the river. Although elaborate charts tell how to compute river ratings, any classification remains essentially subjective:

F: **Flatwater:** Canoe will not drift noticeably with the current. Upstream paddling is easy. Minor obstacles can be easily avoided.

Q: **Quickwater.** The current is strong enough to make paddling upstream difficult. Obstacles can be avoided by careful application of flatwater canoeing techniques.

1:     **Easy rapids.** White water canoeing skills are useful. Rapids may have shallow riffles with only one clear channel or waves which can be run nearly anywhere. Rocks or fallen trees may require dodging in a slow current. Spilled boats can usually be recovered without severe difficulty.

2:     **Medium rapids.** White water canoeing skills are essential. Rapids have waves and/or require rock dodging in a fast current. Ledges have few clear channels. Rescue of spilled boats and boaters may be difficult.

3:     **Difficult rapids.** These should be run only by experienced white water canoeists. Rapids and ledges have intricate routes, large waves, turbulence, and backrollers. Boats may be smashed, pinned so rescue is difficult, or washed downstream. Serious injury to boaters is possible.

Special Difficulties. The chart notes difficulties in excess of the rating assigned to that section, so read the rating column carefully. A section rated 2 does not have any class 2 or even easy class 3 rapids listed under "special difficulties," while a class 1 rapid does receive special attention in a section rated F.

An obstruction marked with an asterisk occurs at the break point and therefore does not require an additional portage for those who start or end a trip at that point.

The current can sweep a canoe under a tree. Paddler should be wearing a lifejacket in fast water!

Fallen trees shift with every rainstorm and often wash great distances downstream, so they can turn up almost anywhere. Only rivers that customarily have extensive fallen trees in a specific area receive special attention in the chart.

WATER LEVEL

The water level depends on the amount of rainfall and varies so much from day to day that it is not possible to predict exactly when a river can be run. Furthermore, the canoeist's water reading skill is more important than a gauge reading in determining the minimum water level required. Experts at handling a boat and reading water can take a loaded canoe down a stretch which others may consider totally unrunnable; this greatly increases the mileage of rivers available for canoeing.

When you are deciding whether the river has enough water to run remember that the water is usually deeper than it appears from the shore. Also, the old poling technique is still useful although disparaged by thrill seekers who wouldn't be caught dead in a shallow river. Some people customarily run shallow riffles while standing and poling with an old 6-foot paddle.

	Even gradient; Sandy or gravel bottom	Even gradient; Larger wastebasket-sized rocks	Drop in chutes around table-sized rocks	Smooth water with ledges or dams
Low Water	Runnable; occasional wading over bars	Unrunnable; just wet rocks	Often one deep channel which can be run with occasional lining	Flatwater; line or portage drops
Medium Water	Class 1 run	Class 2 run	Class 2 run	Quickwater and portage
High Water	Washes out to only a fast current	Washes out to series of waves	Big waves and eddies (class 3)	Chance of being swept over drop; portage greatly lengthened

In general, the faster upper reaches of these rivers require higher water to run than the slower lower reaches, and rapids demand more water than flat stretches. A few sections must be run in medium water usually found only in May or after rainstorms. All but two rivers in this guidebook can be run through an ordinarily wet summer. The water levels of some are totally controlled by dams.

Canoeists have a variety of choices that depend on water conditions. If the lower river is high and muddy, run a stretch further upstream; when the upper parts are too shallow, the flat, lower sections are still available.

The diagram indicates the effect different water levels have on different types of river beds. In each example, the river drops an average of 15 feet per mile.

ACCESS

Good access points are generally mentioned in the text. In theory, any bridge along the highway right-of-way can provide access. In actuality, some are very high with poor footing or have no shoulder for parking and loading or unloading canoes. Access may be possible where the river comes to the road, but the banks frequently are steep and overgrown. State Fish and Game Departments have provided some accesses to some rivers.

Many access points cross private land; in such cases, ask the owners' permission before using them. Obey any specific instructions, and be careful to leave your car where it will not block gates or other cars. Be considerate; a landowner's feelings reflect the behavior of the last group that used his property, and you may have to spend some time searching around and asking permission in advance.

Unfortunately, some take-outs above dams are very difficult, especially in high water. Where access is necessary (for example, by dams) but none is recommended, I could not find a spot worth recommending. In time perhaps, things may change and you might do better.

SCOUTING

Unless your group is very experienced and confident, inspect take-outs and difficult spots before starting the trip. When northern New England was first settled, drops in rivers were the only source of mechanical power. Saw and grist mills were built next to dams at the drops, and frequently towns grew up around them. Bridge engineers had the same requirements as dam builders, a spot narrow for the crossing along with solid rock footings. The demand for bridges was greatest at towns; thus, almost all the rapids and old dams along these rivers are conveniently located underneath bridges in the middle of town. Newer dams have access roads to them.

This makes advance scouting of many difficult spots relatively easy. While spotting cars, you can locate the most suitable place to portage, put in, and take out; and you can ask for necessary permission to cross private property. You can also decide whether to line or run a rapid and where to land if additional scouting should be necessary. Advance scouting also helps the river leader to recognize from above difficult spots which can be hard to visualize from printed instructions, and it can save a lot of walking down the bank. Directions for advance scouting from the road are given in the text.

1 Magalloway River— Umbagog Lake

Miles	Cumulative Miles	Break Points	River Rating	Special Difficulties
	0	Wilson's Mills, Maine		
16			F	
	16	Umbagog Lake		
3¾			F	
	19¾	Errol Landing		Dam*

*Does not require portage if taking out at break point.

MAGALLOWAY RIVER

Remote but easily accessible, the Magalloway River lies north of the White Mountains along the sparsely settled Maine—New Hampshire border. Rising in the timbered hills of the northwest corner of Maine, it flows southward through man-made Aziscoos Lake before turning southwest to cross the border into New Hampshire. Just east of Errol, it joins the Umbagog Lake outlets to form the Androscoggin River. Even the most experienced canoeist may find its upper reaches rough, but the lower portion, from Wilson's Mills in Maine to Errol Dam in New Hampshire, makes an excellent run for a first canoe camping expedition. A side trip around Umbagog Lake, connected to the Magalloway by short, unimpeded channels, is a bonus.

Unlike many northern New England rivers, the Magalloway runs clean, wandering across vast woodland tracts dominated by spruce and fir. The river is placid below Wilson's Mills, and since the dams at Errol and at Aziscoos Lake control water flow, the river can be canoed during the drier months. The James River Company, a major timber interest and landowner around the Magalloway and Umbagog, has established a number of campsites in the area. Many are accessible from the water. The campsites along the Magalloway River and Umbagog Lake are administered by Umbagog Lake Camps on NH 26 at the south end of the lake. For the campsites on the Androscoggin check with Mollidgewock Campground 3 miles south of Errol on NH 16. A use fee is charged.

Wilson's Mills to Umbagog Lake (16 miles).

To put in, drive north from Errol on NH 16 to the bridge at Wilson's Mills, Maine. The river contains difficult rapids upstream but flows

Magalloway River

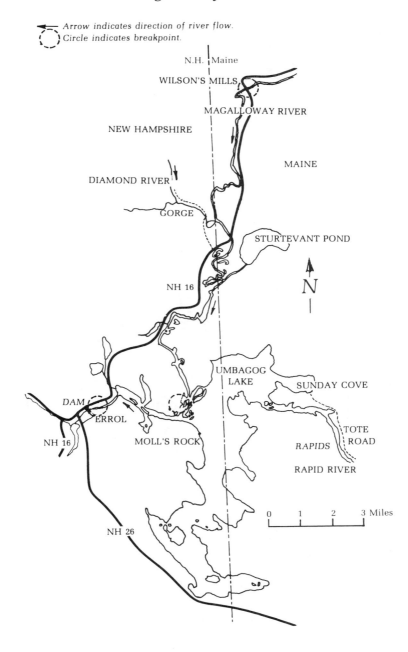

Arrow indicates direction of river flow.
Circle indicates breakpoint.

N.H. Maine

WILSON'S MILLS

MAGALLOWAY RIVER

NEW HAMPSHIRE

MAINE

DIAMOND RIVER

GORGE

STURTEVANT POND

NH 16

N

UMBAGOG
LAKE

SUNDAY COVE

DAM

ERROL

TOTE
ROAD

NH 16

MOLL'S ROCK

RAPIDS

RAPID RIVER

0   1   2   3 Miles

NH 26

smoothly below Wilson's Mills, meandering back and forth through
swamps and oxbow lakes. Although the highway closely follows the
river for much of the way, few houses or other evidence of modern
civilization interrupt the pleasant illusion of a true wilderness region.

The Diamond River, which drains a Dartmouth College land grant,
enters on the right 7 miles (Mi. 7) from Wilson's Mills. The Diamond
cuts through a spectacular gorge about 2 miles from its confluence
with the Magalloway, and you may wish to make a short side trip
here. A private gravel road just east of Wentworth Location on NH 16
will take you to a gate; cars are allowed beyond here only by permit
from Dartmouth College, but pedestrians and cyclists are welcome. A

A rainy lunch stop.

1-mile hike up the road carries you along the cliffs which line the gorge.

Nine miles (Mi. 9) from Wilson's Mills, Sturtevant Pond Outlet flows into the Magalloway from the left. Some campsites in this vicinity are accessible by both car and canoe.

At mile 13, the river starts to swing away from the road in a big marsh-lined loop toward Umbagog Lake. At the end of this 3-mile loop (Mi. 16), a maze of side channels appears to the left. These waterways, which flow through marshes and past numerous small islands, are outlets from Umbagog Lake. In season, white pond lilies thrive in the shallow, slowly moving waters and in places are so thick they reduce the channels' centers to a canoe's width or less and necessitate some pushing and poling.

In former times the Magalloway River and the outlet from Umbagog Lake met to form the Androscoggin River. Now the dam at Errol has raised the water level and flooded out the entire area, so this point can hardly be identified in the maze of channels.

Here, where the river becomes the Androscoggin, you have three choices: to return back up the Magalloway to the take-outs near NH 16, to venture into Umbagog Lake, or to continue a few miles further down the Androscoggin.

Pond lilies and arrowheads.

Umbagog Lake to Errol Landing *(3¾ miles)*.
The short Androscoggin stretch flows leisurely through extensive
marshes formed by ponding behind Errol Dam. Three miles from the
channels to Umbagog you can find a launching ramp on the right
where the river approaches NH 16 (Mi. 19). Take out here, or paddle
another ¾ mile to a second ramp (Mi. 19¾) on the left bank ¼ mile
above Errol Dam.

UMBAGOG LAKE

Nearly 8 miles long and from 1 to 2 miles wide, the relatively shallow
Umbagog straddles the Maine—New Hampshire boundary. Unlike
most of New Hampshire's larger lakes, Umbagog has escaped the
ravages of summer home and recreational development. Its shoreline
presents an almost unbroken vista of woodlands and wetlands set
against a backdrop of fir-studded hills. Moose feed quietly nearby,
ospreys and loons nest along its banks, and brook trout, salmon, and
pickerel swim beneath its surface.

The sparkling blue waters of Umbagog hide another natural

A canoe party explores the lake shore.

resource. On its bottom rests a thick layer of muddy diatomaceous earth, lending credence to the Indian translation of "Umbagog" as "muddy waters." Formed over thousands of years from skeletons of microscopic algae, diatomite is a valuable, silicarich mineral used in a variety of industrial and domestic filtering processes and as an abrasive in cleansers and polishers.

To reach Umbagog Lake, paddle up one of the side channels that lead off from the Magalloway. This brings you to the swampy north-western end of the lake. This side of Umbagog has two established campsites; the first is to the left on one of the small marshy islands which divide the channels. The second, Moll's Rock, is on the western shore 1½ miles south of the outlets and is very popular.

Umbagog's eastern shore is rocky and offers many fine spots for swimming and picnicking. Several attractive campsites are along this shore.

The Rapid River enters Umbagog Lake at its northeastern end. You might want to paddle a couple of miles up this river to the lower end of the rapids. There are campsites on both banks, and a trail up the right bank leads to the dirt tote road that runs between Sunday Cove on Umbagog Lake and Richardson Lake and past the former home of author Louise Dickinson Rich.

The rapids above the campsites provide an excellent opportunity for novices to practice setting, ferrying, and other canoeing skills. They are popular for this purpose, and groups from nearby summer camps often spend whole days here. To run the rapids, unload at one of the campsites and then paddle, track, or carry your canoe upstream as far as you wish.

Instead of returning to the Magalloway to take out, you may paddle to the extreme southern end of Umbagog to the state-owned launching ramp just inside the New Hampshire border on NH 26 east of Errol.

2 Androscoggin River

Miles	Cumulative Miles	Break Points	River Rating	Special Difficulties
	0	Errol Dam		
½			2	
	½	Clear Stream		
3¾			F,Q	
	4¼	Mollidgewock Campground		
4¾			Q,1,2	
	9	Seven Islands Bridge		
9			F,Q	Dam*
	18	Pontook Dam		
3½			Q,2,3	
	21½	Dummer		
9¼			Q,2,3	
	30¾	Berlin		

*Does not require portage if taking out at break point.

The Androscoggin River between Errol and Berlin is one of the most popular—and crowded—canoeing rivers in New Hampshire. It is the only long run in the state with both clean waters and good-sized waves which can dependably be run throughout the summer. The section described here contains three distinct stretches of rapids. The first runs below Errol Dam for ½ mile, the second below Mollidge-wock Campground for 3 miles, and the third below Pontook Dam for about 2 miles. Between these rapid sections are extensive stretches of quickwater and flatwater. Liveries along NH 16 below Errol rent canoes and provide instruction, and several campsites in the area are accessible to both car and canoe.

The rapids of the Androscoggin offer the most thrills for the least investment in skill and money. They are easier than the size of the

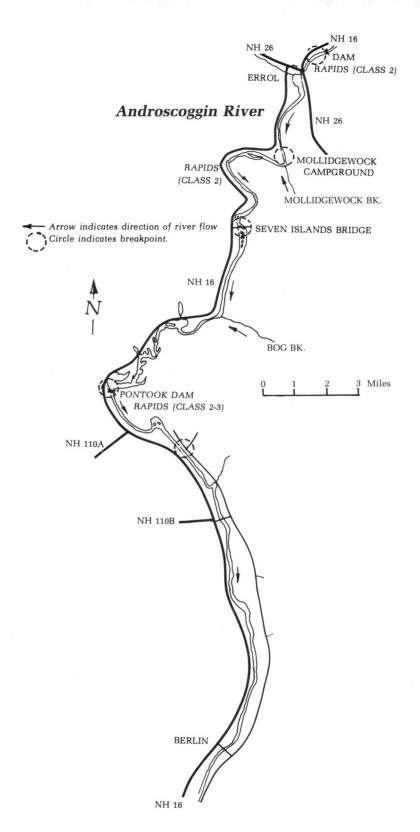

Androscoggin River

NH 16
NH 26
DAM
RAPIDS (CLASS 2)
ERROL
NH 26

MOLLIDGEWOCK
CAMPGROUND

RAPIDS
(CLASS 2)

MOLLIDGEWOCK BK.

← Arrow indicates direction of river flow
Circle indicates breakpoint.

SEVEN ISLANDS BRIDGE

NH 16

N

BOG BK.

0   1   2   3 Miles

PONTOOK DAM
RAPIDS (CLASS 2-3)

NH 110A

NH 110B

BERLIN

NH 16

river and height of the waves might lead you to expect because they are usually run in the summer when the water is warm; this eliminates the very real danger of spills in chilled waters. Because there are few rocks, little skill in maneuvering is required; the rapids are short with good pools below for rescue; and many people are nearby to render assistance should anything go wrong. Also, because the road and your car are normally close by, you do not need to carry your dry pack.

The chief danger of canoeing on the Androscoggin is the false confidence it creates. Although you can safely wash down these

rapids forwards, backwards, or even sideways, people who arrive at the bottom more or less intact think they have learned something about running rapids. When they run afoul of rocks in other rivers, they blame the "lack of water" and not their own lack of skill.

Large lakes and dams keep the water flow on the Androscoggin relatively constant over the season. Minimum flow is only half the average, and the average flow on the Androscoggin would be considered high on most rivers. People used to the Androscoggin often think other rivers are too low because rocks are showing, when in fact they can be dangerously high.

The Androscoggin from Errol to Berlin is seldom run as a canoe camping trip. The standing waves in the rapids tend to fill a loaded canoe, and in any case the campsites along the right bank are readily accessible by car since NH 16 closely follows the river.

While it is possible, and to my mind preferable, to run straight through from Errol Dam to Pontook Dam (it saves a lot of loading and unloading), most people run exclusively either the big rapids or the easier in-between stretches.

Errol Dam to Clear Stream (Rapids) *(½ mile)*.
To run the first set of rapids, put in on the right just below Errol Dam at the pool by NH 16. This ½-mile run consists of two rapids separated by the short pool. To reach the upper rapid, paddle upstream across the pool and carry along the left bank as far as you wish. The rapid below the pool is about ¼ mile long and is crossed about halfway down by the NH 26 bridge. If you are only running rapids, take out on the right in the field just above the mouth of Clear Stream (Mi. ½). There can be a considerable traffic jam here on a good summer weekend.

Clear Stream to Mollidgewock Campground *(3¾ miles)*.
If you are not running the rapids, put in at the take-out by Clear Stream mentioned above. Just under 4 miles of smooth water carry you to a take-out at Mollidgewock Campground (Mi. 4¼), easily spotted on the right.

Mollidgewock Brook enters at the point from the left where the river turns right and the rapids start. Both it and Bog Brook (Mi. 12) offer a mile or more of interesting paddling through a marsh, the distance limited by the paddler's enthusiasm for dragging the canoe up over beaver dams and under bushes.

Mollidgewock Campground to Seven Islands Bridge (Rapids) *(4¾ miles)*.
To run the second set of rapids, put in at Mollidgewock Campground located on a loop of the old highway 3 miles south of Errol. Along the first 3 miles of this section, smooth water alternates with class 2 rapids which have standing waves. The rapids become easier over the last 1¾ miles. Since the road follows the river closely here, you can take out wherever you choose.

Seven Islands Bridge to Pontook Dam *(9 miles)*.
You can select your own put-in along this stretch from NH 16. A class 2
rapid lies under the private Seven Islands Bridge (Mi. 9). Quickwater
follows, becoming slower as you progress downstream. Bog Brook enters
on the left (Mi. 12) opposite a turnout at the sharp turn in NH 16. The
last 5 miles are largely backwater formed by Pontook Dam (Mi. 18). Take
out on the right from a pool adjacent to NH 16, well above the dam.

Pontook Dam to Dummer (Rapids) (3½ miles).
Pontook Dam has been rebuilt for power generation, and the water level
in the rapids is not as reliable as in the upper river. Put in on the right
below the dam. These rapids are the most difficult of the three, with
larger rocks and waves. The rapids run for about 2 miles and are
followed by quickwater. If you are not continuing to Berlin, you can take
out on the right bank (Mi. 20). Stay on the dirt road and don't trample
the hayfield. An alternate take-out is further downstream on the left near
the Dummer-Milan town line (Mi. 21½).

Rafting the boats for a rest.

Dummer to Berlin (9¼ miles).

If you avoided the rapid, put in from an access off a side road on the left bank near the Dummer-Milan town line (Mi. 21½), about 2½ miles above the Milan bridge. This long unobstructed run to Berlin is largely quickwater with occasional riffles. Take out on the right at the recreation area at 27½ miles, or at the playground on the left bank below the first bridge in Berlin (Mi. 30¾).

Below Berlin

River cleanup efforts have greatly improved the quality of the river below Berlin. Therefore, it is now feasible to paddle on the lower parts of the Androscoggin into Maine.

This trip is not continuous to the trip above due to the dams in Berlin. Put in at the bridge in Shelburne where the Appalachian Trail crosses the Androscoggin River. The river is a pleasant class 1, gradually becoming quickwater, and then slowing down. Occasionally an easy rapid appears. There are mountain views across open meadows. It is 36 miles to Rumford Point, with no obstructions; the first dam is 3 miles further at Rumford. There is a campsite on the river at Bethel, halfway down.

3   Baker River

Miles	Cumulative Miles	Break Points	River Rating	Special Difficulties
	0	Wentworth		
6			1	
	6	West Rumney		
4			Q, 1	Cl 2 rapid
	10	Rumney		
10½			Q	
	20½	Plymouth		

The Baker River rises in the White Mountains near the summit of Mount Moosilauke and flows south and then east to join the Pemigewasset River at Plymouth. It is a small, clear mountain stream going into Wentworth, where it then slows down and begins to meander across the valley floor. While it is more popular during the spring months in high water, it can also be run in a normally wet summer. Its banks are largely wooded, with occasional houses along the way. The Baker is often used for float trips by students from Plymouth State College and is a good river to run in combination with the lower Pemigewasset.

Although the Baker was followed by Indians on their way to Montreal and was undoubtedly known also to white trappers, its existence was not recorded until 1712, when Lieutenant Thomas Baker led an expedition of thirty-two men up the Connecticut River to the small settlements near Haverhill and then returned down the river that now bears his name.

The Baker was an important link in the early colonial route from the New Hampshire seacoast to the northern settlements along the Connecticut. The original trail led north past Lake Winnipesaukee through Sandwich Notch to Campton on the Pemigewasset and then up the Baker River valley. In 1764, construction was authorized for the Coos Road which ran from Haverhill down the Baker valley to the coastal region. This first road to New Hampshire's northern settlements was completed in 1767. Forty years later, in 1804, a survey party exploring the alternate and higher route through Franconia Notch discovered the Old Man of the Mountain.

Baker River

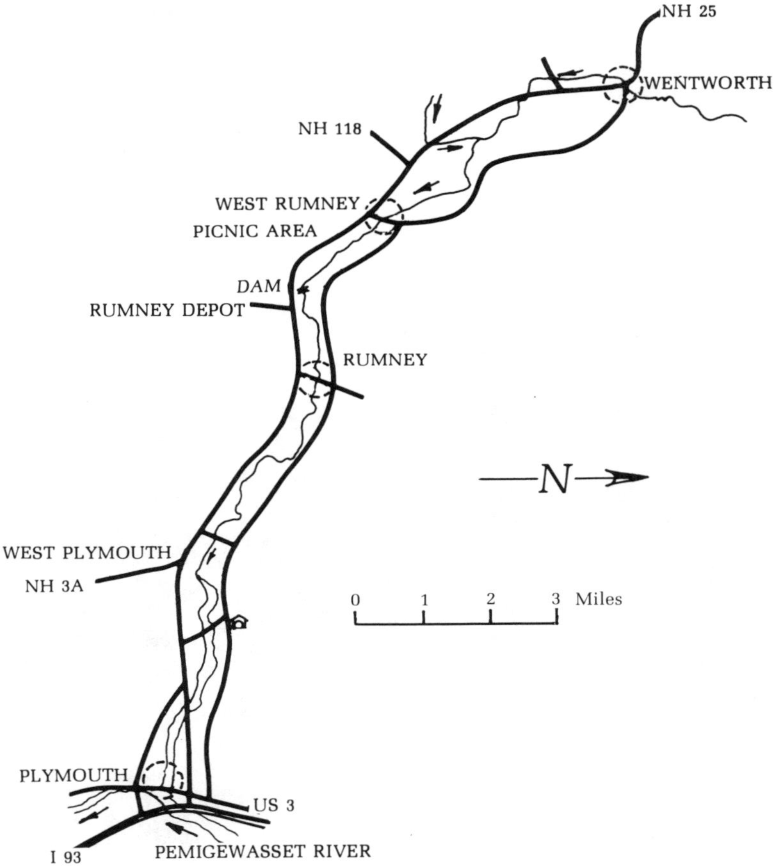
NH 25
WENTWORTH
NH 118
WEST RUMNEY
PICNIC AREA
DAM
RUMNEY DEPOT
RUMNEY
N
WEST PLYMOUTH
NH 3A
0 1 2 3 Miles
PLYMOUTH
US 3
I 93
PEMIGEWASSET RIVER

Arrow indicates direction of river flow.
Circle indicates breakpoint.

Wentworth to West Rumney *(6 miles).*
The ball park off NH 25 on the left bank below the bridge at
Wentworth is a convenient place to begin a trip down the Baker
River, although in low water this 6-mile stretch is too shallow and
rocky to run. The Baker passes beneath a small bridge across a narrow
gorge (Mi. 1¼) and the NH 25 bridge (Mi. 2) before reaching West
Rumney (Mi. 6).

West Rumney to Rumney *(4 miles).*
In low water when the preceding stretch cannot be run, put in below
the steel bridge at West Rumney. Here the Baker becomes deeper
and slower, and while you may have to wade occasionally, the clear
water and sandy, rocky bottom invite swimming in any case.

A highway picnic area with some facilities and good parking also
offers access 1¼ miles further downstream. Another ½ mile brings
you to the remains of a 3-foot dam which lies around a blind corner
to the left (Mi. 7¾). A short class 2 rapid is below it. The right bank
with a visible gauging station is the best side on which to line or carry.
A fast current continues for 2¼ miles to the bridge to Rumney (Mi. 10).

Flowering bushes line the banks in spring at the washed-out dam.

Rumney to Plymouth *(10¼ miles)*.

You can avoid the rapid by putting in at the Rumney bridge. The Baker continues to flow quickly past low cutbanks through rural countryside with excellent views of Stinson Mountain to the north. The covered bridge (Mi. 16) 6 miles below Rumney has a steel guard to prevent vehicles that are too high from crossing; this bridge offers good access, but the high NH 25 bridge further downstream (Mi. 18½) does not. The current becomes slower over the last 3 miles. The best take-out at Plymouth is on the right, upstream of the US 3 bridge (Mi. 20¼), where a dirt track leads to the river. A railroad bridge crosses just below the US 3 bridge, and the current picks up again over the short distance to the Pemigewasset (Mi. 20½).

Many people prefer to wear their vest style lifejacket under their rainjacket. It is warmer, more comfortable and allows easy removal of rainjacket after shower.

4   *Pemigewasset River*

Miles	Cumulative Miles	Break Points	River Rating	Special Difficulties
	0	Plymouth		
16			F,Q	Dam*
	16	Ayers Island Dam		
1½			2,3	
	17½	Below Bristol Bridge		
10½			F,Q,1	Dam*
	28	Franklin Falls Dam		
2½			F,2	Dam
	30½	Winnipesaukee River		

*Does not require portage if taking out at break point.

The Pemigewasset River rises in Franconia Notch, flows south to the Winnipesaukee River in Franklin, and becomes the Merrimack. The upper river can be run only in very high water, but along most of its length below Plymouth, where the Baker joins the Pemigewasset, canoeing is possible almost anytime. The one exception is the 1½-mile stretch immediately below Ayers Island Dam, 16 miles south of Plymouth.

The origin of the name "Pemigewasset" is unclear. One theory is that it came from the Indian words *penaquil* (crooked), *wadchu* (mountain), *cooash* (pine), and *auke* (place), which different sources variously render as "crooked pine place in the mountains", "crooked mountain pine place", and so forth, depending on the arrangement of the words. A euphonious, if not especially accurate, translation is "valley of the winding water among the mountain pines." A simpler theory is that invading Abnaki Indians named it in honor of their leader against the Iroquois.

Pemigewasset River - part 1

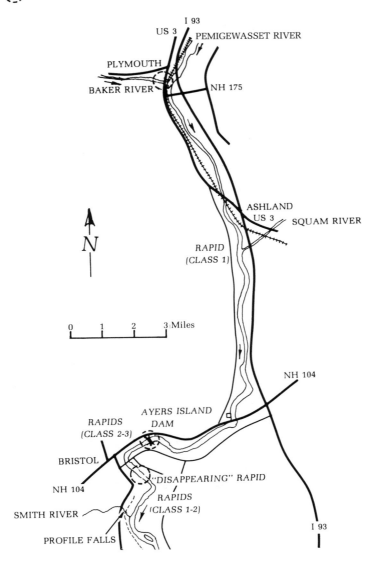

Arrow indicates direction of river flow.
Circle indicates breakpoint.

I 93
US 3
PEMIGEWASSET RIVER
PLYMOUTH
BAKER RIVER
NH 175
N
ASHLAND
US 3
SQUAM RIVER
RAPID
(CLASS 1)
0 1 2 3 Miles
NH 104
AYERS ISLAND
DAM
RAPIDS
(CLASS 2-3)
BRISTOL
"DISAPPEARING" RAPID
NH 104
RAPIDS
(CLASS 1-2)
SMITH RIVER
I 93
PROFILE FALLS

Pemigewasset River - part 2

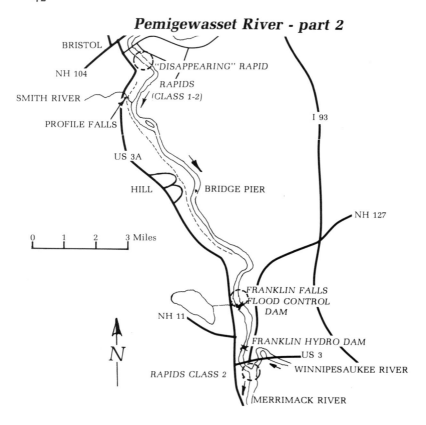

BRISTOL

NH 104

"DISAPPEARING" RAPID

RAPIDS
(CLASS 1-2)

SMITH RIVER

PROFILE FALLS

I 93

US 3A

HILL   BRIDGE PIER

NH 127

0   1   2   3 Miles

FRANKLIN FALLS
FLOOD CONTROL
DAM

NH 11

N

FRANKLIN HYDRO DAM
US 3

RAPIDS CLASS 2   WINNIPESAUKEE RIVER

MERRIMACK RIVER

Plymouth to Ayers Island Dam *(16 miles).*

One put-in is from the right bank of the Baker River at the end of a
dirt track just above the US 3 bridge at Plymouth. It is ¼ mile to the
confluence with the Pemigewasset and another ¼ mile down the
Pemigewasset to the NH 175 bridge. The banks to Ayers Island are
heavily wooded; no roads follow the river closely, so you see few
houses.

When the Ayers Island Dam is full, its backwater extends nearly the
full 16 miles to Plymouth. Under these conditions, the river slows
down and deepens as it makes its way toward the dam. The high US
3 bridge (Mi.5½) west of Ashland offers poor access. Just below the
mouth of Squam River (Mi. 7½), an easy class 2 rapid straddles a small
island. A launching ramp (Mi. 13½) on the right just above the NH
104 bridge offers access. Take out here or 2½ miles further
downstream on the right above the Ayers Island Dam (Mi. 16). The
dam lies just off NH 104.

One of my experiences with this stretch provides a classic example of why you should never unconditionally accept a river descripton given by anybody or any guidebook, including this one. Five different friends, each of whom had made the trip many times, swore on a stack of life jackets that the preceding description was correct, and it also agreed with AMC and Burmeister guidebooks. What better place to take a couple of novices for a canoeing lesson!

The river did look a bit low when we parked our second car, but I had the description on unimpeachable authority and was more interested in making sure necessities were in the other car than in

Running the inside of the curve at "Disappearing Rapid."

inspecting the river. The first half of the trip had more current than I expected and extensive mud flats. When the "easy" class 2 rapid below Squam River heralded its approach with a roar of white water, I realized something was amiss—the dam had just been drawn down! Conditions here are quite different when the dam has been emptied.

There was no convenient escape route, and my memory of the contours here was that the total drop was no more than 30 feet, of which we had already made 5 feet. This worked out to an average drop of only 5 feet per mile, so I chose to continue. However, inexperienced canoeists, anticipating the easier run when the dam is full, could have been in serious difficulty.

A river slowing down above a dam deposits sediment evenly over the bottom. Thus, when the channel widened, there was not enough water to float the canoe. The silt in suspension was like quicksand; we sank above our knees and had great difficulty pulling out. For the same reason, it was impossible to pole our way down. By fast footwork—easing out, shoving the canoe sideways, and jumping back in quickly—we managed to pass the shallow spots.

Beyond another set of rapids, the river was cutting through even thicker layers of accumulated sediment. The suspended matter was reminiscent of the Colorado River, while the narrow channel caused standing waves. And every so often, a yard or two of material sliding into the river from the unstable cliffs on the right would produce more waves.

We were relieved to see the NH 104 bridge and our take-out, but the fun was not yet over. The launching ramp by the bridge was still 30 unstable feet above our heads. A pie-in-the-face style comedian could have made a good routine out of our efforts to drag the canoe—and ourselves—up the wet, slippery mud bank.

Ayers Island Dam to below Bristol Bridge (1½ miles).

If you are running the 1½-mile stretch of rapids below Ayers Island Dam and are hand carrying the dam, follow a trail down the hill to a sewage treatment plant surrounded by a chain link fence, and then carry straight over to the river. This access can also be reached by car down a road adjacent to the dam.

The rapids may not be runnable when the dam is closed, and when it is open, they are a rocky class 2 to 3, even 4 in heavy water, and a successful run requires considerable skill. The left may be a better side to run along the upper part, and the most difficult drops are midway to the Bristol bridge (Mi. 17).

I had been collecting information on this stretch for quite some time before running it myself. All my sources agreed that the 1-mile run from the dam to the Britsol bridge was class 2 to 3 in low water and even worse in high water. However, the ½-mile stretch below the bridge produced conflicting stories. Some said the rapids were easier,

Paddles used for portage yoke. Tuck up painter to avoid tripping.

some said they ended together, while others claimed a very difficult drop with high standing waves made the rapids impossible to run in an open canoe without swamping. Ratings ran from class 1 to class 4.

The "disappearing" rapid lies around a sweeping bend in the river below the bridge. Inexperienced canoeists and wave enthusiasts who follow the current around the outside of the curve encounter a long line of standing waves where the current hits a rocky ledge. The water here is deep with a good run-out into flattish water, so someone who doesn't mind taking in water may find this side of the rapid exciting to run.

On the other hand, experienced canoeists approaching prudently on the inside of the bend need only dodge a few rocks, and would scarcely notice the waves on the far side of the river. When low water makes the inside too rocky, you can run a line of smooth water adjacent to the waves.

Scouts from Mead Wilderness Base use the Pemigewasset from Squam River to Manchester on the Merrimack as one of their adventure canoe trips. I wondered how a group of relatively inexperienced boys would make out in the notorious Bristol rapids, so one day I went and watched them; they did very well indeed. The secret of their success was knowing how to reach shore. They did not attempt to run the worst drops but would paddle a little in the easier parts, set over to shore, line a bit, carry a bit around a particularly bad drop, and so on. The leaders knew the river and knew the boys' capabilities, and they ran the rapids without mishap. Since they were carrying duffle, they lined their canoes around an overflow channel on the right at the "disappearing" rapid.

Below Bristol Bridge to Franklin Falls Dam *(10½ miles).*
A side road on the left bank offers access below the big rapids around Bristol (Mi. 17½). Short bits of fast water and occasional rocks appear over the next couple of miles to the mouth of the Smith River (Mi. 19½), but beyond that, the water gradually becomes slower and deeper. The possible ponding area of the Franklin Falls flood control dam extends back to the Bristol bridge. No camping is permitted in the impoundment area, although day use is allowed.

Old NH 3A, which is still passable, offers access at several places. One of the best is near the old bridge at Hill, where piers are still clearly visible (Mi. 23½).

The approach to Franklin Falls Dam (Mi. 28) poses no problems. It can be seen ½ mile away and like most flood control dams, is drawn down at times when you would want to canoe. In addition, a log boom well above the dam shunts logs, debris, and canoeists into the left bank. The dam area is clearly visible from NH 3A on the right, but the only access is from NH 127 on the left. Watch for a sign 2 miles north of Franklin. If you receive permission to drive through the gate and down to the water, the take-out here is easy, and unless you plan to continue down the Merrimack, this would be a likely spot to end your trip. Keep your vehicle on the hard road; the ground by the water is soft, and odds and ends of debris (such as boards with sharp nails) are scattered around.

Franklin Falls Dam to Winnipesaukee River *(2½ miles).*
To put in below the dam, continue down the dirt road noted above to the water. The total portage is ¾ mile. After 1½ miles, you reach the Franklin Hydroelectric Dam (Mi. 29½), which should be portaged on the right. NH 3A gives access here below the dam. Class 2 rapids continue for 1 mile under the US 3 bridge in Franklin to the confluence with the Winnipesaukee and the start of the Merrimack River (Mi. 30½).

5   Merrimack River

Miles	Cumulative Miles	Break Points	River Rating	Special Difficulties
	0	Winnipesaukee River		
17			F,Q,1	
	17	Sewall's Falls Road		
4½			Q,2	see text
	21½	Concord		
20¾			F,Q	2 dams
	42¼	Manchester		Dam*
11¼			F,Q,2	2 ledges (class 3)
	54	Merrimack		
7¼			F,Q	
	61¼	Nashua		

*Does not require portage if taking out at break point.

The Merrimack River begins where the Pemigewasset and Winnipesaukee Rivers join in Franklin. Flowing south through central New
Hampshire, it passes Concord, the state capital, and heavily in-
dustrialized Manchester and Nashua before entering Massachusetts.
There, it turns northeast, runs parallel to the New Hampshire border,
and reaches the Atlantic Ocean at Newburyport. Like many big rivers
draining northern New England, the Merrimack was once a major
route to the interior for Indians, early colonists, and commercial
steamboat companies. The river current is generally slow, and the
water is usually high enough to run throughout the summer. The
towns along the Merrimack have followed the construction of sewage
treatment plants with an upsurge of interest in the river, and many
new parks and accesses have been built, with more in the planning
stage. The upper stretches combine well with camping trips taken
down the Baker and Pemigewasset Rivers.

Merrimack River - part 1

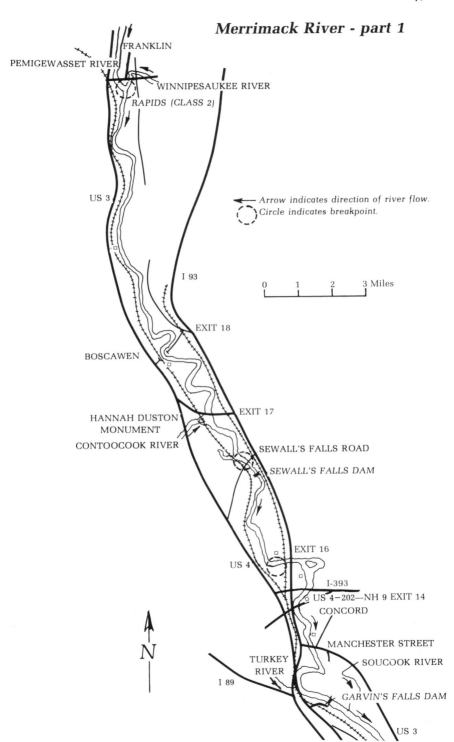

FRANKLIN

PEMIGEWASSET RIVER

WINNIPESAUKEE RIVER

RAPIDS (CLASS 2)

US 3

Arrow indicates direction of river flow.
Circle indicates breakpoint.

0   1   2   3 Miles

I 93

EXIT 18

BOSCAWEN

EXIT 17

HANNAH DUSTON
MONUMENT

CONTOOCOOK RIVER

SEWALL'S FALLS ROAD

SEWALL'S FALLS DAM

EXIT 16

US 4

I-393

US 4-202--NH 9 EXIT 14

CONCORD

MANCHESTER STREET

SOUCOOK RIVER

TURKEY
RIVER

I 89

GARVIN'S FALLS DAM

N

US 3

Winnipesaukee River to Sewall's Falls Road *(17 miles).*
A good put-in for a trip down the Merrimack is located on the east
side of the Winnipesaukee River. The Franklin High School occupies
the point of land between the rivers. Take the road south from US 3
just across the bridge. In a quarter mile put in from a dirt track. The
banks are wooded along the ¼-mile run to the Pemigewasset and the
start of the Merrimack.

The first 2 miles on the Merrimack have four short, class 1 rapids.
The water is clear and pleasant, flowing through woodlands inter-
rupted by an occasional cornfield or house. Much of the left bank
belongs to the Gold Star Sod Farm, and you can sometimes hear traffic from nearby roads.

People wishing an easier start or a short trip can use the launching
ramp 6 miles south of Franklin, which is below the rapids. It is
reached by car from US 3. Take the dirt track just north of the
Merrimack County buildings. The bridge at Boscawen (Mi. 10¾) is
closed but offers access to the river at both ends. To reach the left end
of the bridge opposite the town, take exit 18 from I-93 west down a
very steep hill to the river. A park is on the right downstream of the
bridge, with a launching ramp at its southern end.

The river bottom is clean and sandy, and the river meanders
pleasantly past high cutbanks. Near Penacook, the high bridge (Mi.
15) connecting I-93 (exit 17) to US 3-4 crosses the Merrimack just
above the old bridge, only half of which still remains. The right half,
which belonged to Boscawen, was sold for scrap.

Immediately below, the Contoocook River enters from the right. On
the small island in the river's mouth stands a monument to Hannah
Duston, who was captured by Indians from her home in Haverhill,
Massachusetts, and carried up the river toward Canada. During the
night of March 30, 1697, Hannah Duston, her midwife, and a
fourteen-year-old boy scalped their sleeping captors and escaped at
the crack of dawn by canoe back down the Merrimack. While their
trip upstream had taken ten days, their journey to safety required only
two. Both trips must have been exceedingly difficult and chilly, as the
river runs high in March and is still clogged by ice floes. A friend and I
wondered which of the three had the skill to run the many rapids; the
dams, of course, had not been built, but certainly the Hooksett and
Amoskeag falls could not have been run even then, and the other
rapids would have required considerable canoeing knowledge to
negotiate. My son pointed out that it took us more than two days (in
early April) to travel the distance the three made in only one, but then
they did have a strong incentive and a very early start!

Access to the river from the ''park and ride'' and parking for the
island is poor. Lowering the water level at the dam has caused an easy
rapid to appear just above Sewall's Falls Bridge. Good access is avail-

able here on the right below the bridge where a car can be driven almost to the water (Mi. 17).

Sewall's Falls Road to Concord *(4½ miles).*
The largest log crib dam in the country was breached in the spring of 1984 (Mi. 18). This caused the river to drop to its natural level in medium and low water and exposed the class 2 rapids from just above Sewall's Falls bridge to the dam. At present the whole stretch, including the breach in the dam, can be run. A recreation area is planned, with access to both above and below the dam site.

A few riffles continue below the dam, and then the river is smooth to the first of the ramps in Concord, at exit 16 (Mi. 20¾).

Concord to Manchester *(20¾ miles).*
Concord has four launching ramps. The first, on the left bank upstream of the railroad bridge, is just above the I-93 bridge. This access can be reached from exit 16 of I-93. Exit west, and turn left at the T intersection toward the river. The Society for the Protection of NH

Remains of Sewalls Falls Dam

Forests is high on the left side of the river below the bridge. At the large island it is 2 miles to the right and 3 miles around the left to the launching ramp just above the I-393 bridge. Along this stretch are numerous muskrats and birds. Below the I-393 bridge cutbanks tower above the river on the left. The Morton State Office and State Supreme Court buildings overlook the river here.

The third launching ramp (Mi. 24½) is on the left bank just above the Bridge Street bridge, at exit 14 of I-93. The skyline of Concord with the Capitol dome rises on the right.

The fourth launching ramp (Mi. 26) lies in a deep cove on the left above a picnic area upstream of the Manchester Street bridge, which carries US 3 to exit 13 of I-93. This bridge crosses the river at an angle with its piers perpendicular to the roadway and diagonal to the river flow, so they create considerable turbulence. (Most new bridges have piers parallel to the river flow, regardless of the angle the bridge itself makes.) Further downstream, where NH 3A comes close to the river, the inundated Turkey Falls at the mouth of the Turkey River also cause some turbulence.

Shortly beyond, a building on the right and an abutment on the left mark the Garvin's Falls Dam (Mi. 29½). Land just above the dam on the left for an easy carry. This is a possible access since a heavy duty vehicle can drive down a dirt track nearly to the top of the dam. Ordinary cars can drive on the right to a fair spot to launch.

The current along the 17-mile run to Manchester depends on the height of the water. Both the Soucook River (Mi. 30¼), just beyond Garvin's Falls, and the Suncook River (Mi. 33¼), 3 miles downstream, enter from the left. Two launching ramps are on the left, one above and one below the Suncook River.

Except for the town of Suncook, high on a hill to the left, the banks along this stretch show little sign of civilization.

On the right shore overlooking Hooksett stands the "interesting mountain" noted by Thoreau in *A Week on the Concord and Merrimack.* The view from this knob more than justifies the easy climb. Follow NH 3A north from the bridge in Hooksett to the first street on the left and take the first left off this street. The trail to the summit starts at the circle at the end of the street.

After the "mountain" comes into view, start watching for the Hooksett Dam (Mi. 35), which lies above the Hooksett bridge and is not easy to see in advance. Take out at the launching ramp in the eddy on the left. A confident canoeist who is hand carrying in low water may continue along the left shore and take out just below the old bridge abutment. Carry down the paved road past the power station and parking area to another launching ramp.

You should exercise care at the river bend below Hooksett Dam, where you find an assortment of piers from an old bridge, a new bridge, and a railroad bridge. Halfway to Manchester, the I-93 bridge

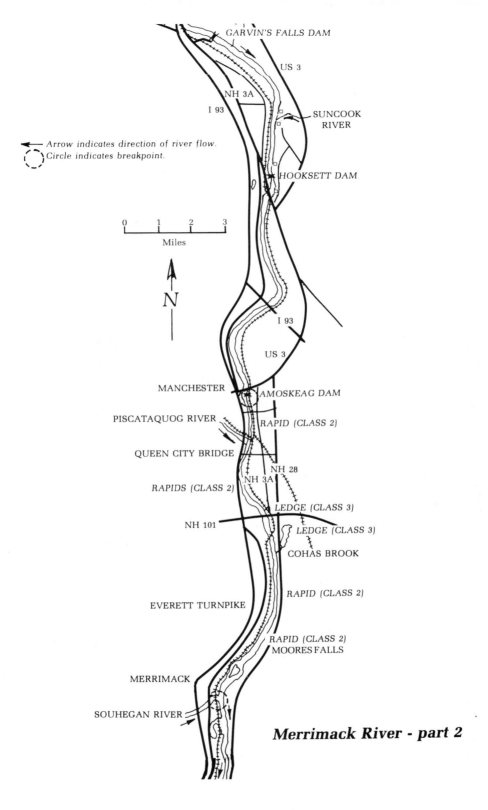

GARVIN'S FALLS DAM

US 3

NH 3A

I 93

SUNCOOK RIVER

Arrow indicates direction of river flow.
Circle indicates breakpoint.

HOOKSETT DAM

0   1   2   3
Miles

N

I 93

US 3

MANCHESTER
AMOSKEAG DAM

PISCATAQUOG RIVER
RAPID (CLASS 2)

QUEEN CITY BRIDGE

NH 28
NH 3A

RAPIDS (CLASS 2)

LEDGE (CLASS 3)

NH 101
LEDGE (CLASS 3)

COHAS BROOK

RAPID (CLASS 2)

EVERETT TURNPIKE

RAPID (CLASS 2)
MOORES FALLS

MERRIMACK

SOUHEGAN RIVER

Merrimack River - part 2

crosses, but the banks are surprisingly wild until the last mile above
the city. The paddle past the suburbs of Manchester is interesting for
its view of houses, retaining walls, and piers along the banks. Take out
on the right by a good parking area just above the high Amoskeag
Bridge (Mi. 42¾) to carry Amoskeag Dam.

Manchester to Merrimack *(11¼) miles.*

You can survey the rapids through Manchester both from the bridges
and from the northbound lane of the Manchester bypass on the west
bank (a link in the Everett Turnpike). Below the dam, factory walls
rise sheer from the left side of the river, while the highway runs
along a high bank on the right, but the noise of the water drowns out
other sounds. The dam controls the water level here, and the run is
easiest in fairly high water when a canoe can slide smoothly along
the right bank. A practice slalom course is being designed for this
area. The rapid decrease as you pass through Manchester, ending

Erosion forms intricate patterns in the layers of sand, clay and rock.

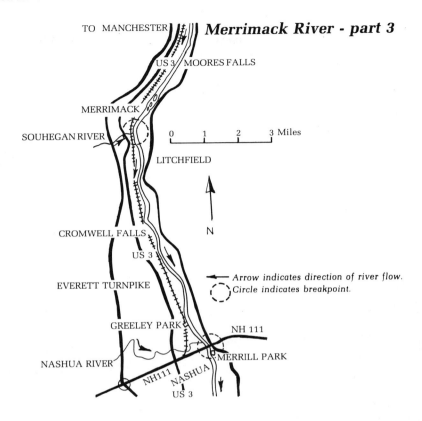

TO MANCHESTER

Merrimack River - part 3

US 3 / MOORES FALLS

MERRIMACK

SOUHEGAN RIVER

0   1   2   3 Miles

LITCHFIELD

N

CROMWELL FALLS

US 3

EVERETT TURNPIKE

Arrow indicates direction of river flow.
Circle indicates breakpoint.

GREELEY PARK   NH 111

NASHUA RIVER   MERRILL PARK

NH111   NASHUA
US 3

with fast water. The two riverside parks offer very poor access.

Back in the early 1800s a canal made it possible for boats to float all the way to Hooksett. This boat canal was not the mill canal which was at the level of Canal Street and has now been mostly filled in, but down at river level. One remaining part which can be identified is on the left above the Granite Street bridge; from the shore it can be seen upstream of Loeb Park. An alert canoeist can spot remnants of it at several of the rapids.

The Piscataquog River comes in from the right just above Queen City Bridge (Mi. 45).

One and one-half miles below Queen City Bridge you reach an easy riffle, and 1 mile below that, just beyond an island, the high NH 101 bridge (Mi. 47½). The class 3 ledge below can be run on either side, but not down the middle. A new pipe across the river makes this drop more difficult than it formerly was. The ledge ¾ mile beyond, under the railroad bridge, is best run on the left at most water stages. It can be inspected from side roads on either side. Shortly past this last ledge, Cohas Brook on the left cascades down Goff's Falls into the Merrimack.

If you have run the rapids this far, you need not inspect the next two rapids. The first lies 1 mile below Cohas Brook beyond an island. The second rapid, Moores Falls (Mi. 51¼), is much longer and lies below the second power line crossing. The right is usually a better side to run. Access is difficult along this stretch, since the few roads which come close to the river are on a high bank. Take out from the Souhegan River (Mi. 54), which enters from the right, in the town of Merrimack.

Merrimack to Nashua *(7¼ miles).*
Most of this distance the river flows with a slow current. Only at Cromwells Falls does it speed up. On the right side is one of the few recognizable sections of the canal that used to bypass all the falls on the river.

In Nashua there is access at Greeley Park, where a boat ramp is to be built on the right. Access is also possible below the NH 111 bridge on the left at Merrill Park.

High eroded banks opposite sand bar.

6 Batten Kill

Miles	Cumulative Miles	Break Points	River Rating	Special Difficulties
	0	Hard Bridge		
5			F,Q	
	5	US 7 Bridge		
2			Q,2	
	7	Arlington		
20½			Q,1	Small dam
	27½	East Greenwich, New York		

The Batten Kill in southwestern Vermont is a beautiful, clear tributary of the Hudson River, and much of it can be run throughout a normally wet summer. Rising just north of Manchester, it flows southward along the Vermont Valley, sandwiched between the Green Mountains on the east and Mount Equinox on the west. From Arlington, where it turns abruptly west, it breaks through the Taconic Range to enter New York State, swinging south and then north in a wide S-shaped loop before joining the Hudson.

Spanned by four covered bridges, the sparkling waters of the Batten Kill tempt swimmers on a warm summer day, brook trout entice fishermen to try their luck, and a fair but easy current speeds canoeists along their way. Below Manchester, only one place could cause problems for the less skillful paddler. You can avoid this by starting instead at Arlington. From here, the river offers an easy 20-mile run in predominantly class 1 water. Two private campgrounds front the river, one north of Arlington and the other on the southern loop near Shushan, New York.

The first 2¾ miles from Union Street in Manchester to the bridge on Richville Road is narrow, shallow and badly obstructed with fallen trees. Therefore, it is better to start at the next bridge below Manchester.

Hard Bridge to US 7A Bridge *(5 miles).*

This stretch is less rocky than the previous section and holds fewer fallen trees and other obstructions. Surrounding countryside is mostly devoted to farming, with the land posted along much of the right bank and some of the left.

Below Sunderland, the current slows down somewhat, (Mi. 3) and the river deepens. The 2-mile run to the US 7A bridge (Mi. 5) is pleasant, with some quickwater, some flatwater, and occasional riffles.

US 7A Bridge to Arlington *(2 miles).*

You can put in or take out at the US 7A bridge. A trail leads down to the river from a parking area on the left bank just below the bridge. Still relatively deep, the Batten Kill continues to flow slowly for a little over 1 mile. The current picks up just below the mouth of Roaring Branch (Mi. 6), a side stream entering from the left. The river swings left, and a huge boulder sits toward the shore on the right. The rapid here is scratchy in low water, and in high water creates sizable waves (class 2 or possibly class 3). You may want to line or carry this rapid on the right. A private campground is just below the rapid on the left.

Easy rapids continue for another ½ mile. At Arlington, VT 313 crosses (Mi. 6¼); a good parking area is on the left above the bridge.

Arlington to East Greenwich, N.Y. *(20½ miles).*

The old dam half a mile downstream is almost gone and presents no problem, except for a few riffles. A canoe livery is located at the bridge below. Here the Batten Kill turns sharply west to leave the

Lifting over a fallen tree.

Batten Kill River

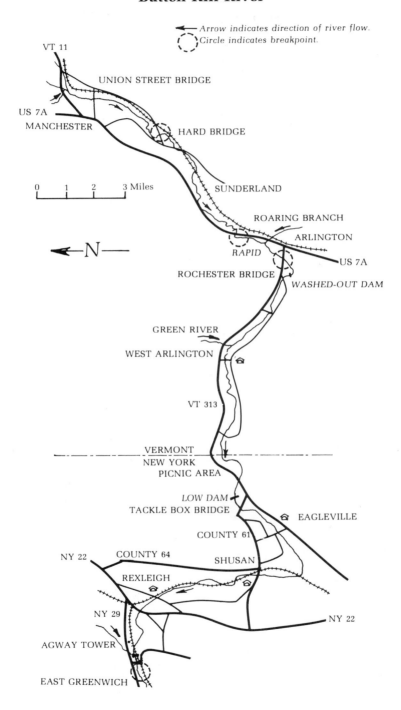

Arrow indicates direction of river flow.
Circle indicates breakpoint.

VT 11

UNION STREET BRIDGE

US 7A
MANCHESTER

HARD BRIDGE

0   1   2   3 Miles

SUNDERLAND

ROARING BRANCH

ARLINGTON

←N—

RAPID

US 7A

ROCHESTER BRIDGE

WASHED-OUT DAM

GREEN RIVER

WEST ARLINGTON

VT 313

VERMONT
NEW YORK
PICNIC AREA

LOW DAM
TACKLE BOX BRIDGE

EAGLEVILLE

COUNTY 61

NY 22   COUNTY 64

SHUSAN

REXLEIGH

NY 29

NY 22

AGWAY TOWER

EAST GREENWICH

Vermont Valley and flows through the breach in the Taconic Range. For the next 20 miles, the river gradient drops almost evenly, and a fast current riffles over small rocks giving a smooth, pleasing ride. This lower portion can be run in all but the driest summers, which may explain its popularity for float trips. Canoes find themselves sharing waters with all manner of craft, from fancy rubber rafts to inner tubes and air mattresses, and even an occasional log! With very litle effort, you can cover the first 5 miles to the Arlington Green Bridge in about three hours. Less than 1 mile above the covered bridge, the milky green waters of the aptly named Green River (Mi. 11¼) join the Batten Kill.

The Arlington Green Bridge, built in the 1850s, is the first of four covered bridges that cross the lower portion of the Batten Kill. Bridges appear regularly every couple of miles from here to Shushan.

Just across the New York State line a picinic area on the right offers a fair access. Below it log cribs extend out from the right bank, and a hill rises almost vertically on the left. The cribs were built recently to stabilize the shore and to improve fishing conditions. Both banks are posted against any use other than fishing access. The NY 313 bridge crosses at Mi. 14¾. The low dam just above the County 61 bridge (Mi. 16¼), called the Tackle Box Bridge in reference to a former bait shop, can be run.

The river loops south in a giant arc around huge rocky cliffs before flowing north to Shushan. The mountains here consist of complex layers of different types of rock which have been subjected to

Rexleigh covered bridge.

repeated uplifting and folding. Erosional forces of glaciers and ancient streams have carved away the exposed weaker rock, leaving gaps and breaches in the mountain ridge. Today's Batten Kill, following the path of least resistance, flows around the harder structures left behind.

The old covered bridge at Eagleville (Mi. 17¼) still carries traffic, but the one at Shushan (Mi. 21¼) is now a local historical museum. It still stands in place, but its original purpose is now served by a newer bridge located immediately upstream. A private campground is on the left about halfway between these two bridges, just before the County 64 bridge.

North of Shushan a railroad crosses and recrosses the Batten Kill. Near the height of its northern loop, an old mill (Mi. 25½) still stands although the dam that powered it has completely washed away. Immediately beyond, you pass beneath the fourth covered bridge. On warm days, watch for children leaping into the river from a hole in the bridge's siding. When the bridge was rebuilt in 1984, an "inspection door" was left in the wall.

Another ¾ mile brings you to the NY 22 bridge (Mi. 26¾). You then pass yet another railroad bridge, and a tall cement Agway tower is visible on the right as you approach East Greenwich. Black Creek (Mi. 27) enters the Batten Kill here on the right. The dam at East Greenwich is gone now. Best access is a quarter mile below the bridge on the right.

The river continues much the same for another 6 miles to Battenville, N.Y.

Rebuilt bridge showing "Inspection Door."

7   Otter Creek

Miles	Cumulative Miles	Break Points	River Rating	Special Difficulties
	0	South Wallingford		
5¾			Q,1,2	
	5¾	Wallingford		
15½			1,Q	
	21¼	Rutland		
1¼			F,Q,2	2 dams
	22½	Center Rutland		
7			F	Dam*
	29½	Proctor		
38			Q	Dam*
	67½	Middlebury		
12¼			F,Q,2	4 dams
	79¾	Lemon Fair		

*Does not require portage if taking out at break point.

Vermont's longest river, Otter Creek, rises west of the Green Mountain range only a few miles north of the source of the Batten Kill, one of the few New England rivers that flows northward for its entire length. It empties into Lake Champlain north of Vergennes.

Almost all of Otter Creek's canoeable stretches are quickwater with no rapids, since the river's drop is largely concentrated in unrunnable waterfalls, the sites of which are now occupied by dams. Mountain views from the river are lovely, and even shuttling cars is delightfully scenic.

Although you can run Otter Creek from Danby or above after a rain when the water is high and muddy further downstream, for most of the season it is better to begin at Wallingford or Center Rutland. These runs offer pleasant, easy paddling.

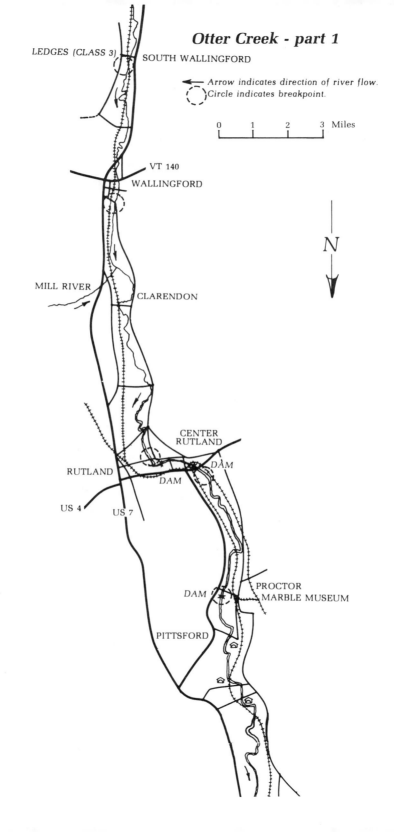

Otter Creek - part 1

LEDGES (CLASS 3)   SOUTH WALLINGFORD

→ *Arrow indicates direction of river flow.*
⟲ *Circle indicates breakpoint.*

0 1 2 3 Miles

VT 140

WALLINGFORD

N

MILL RIVER

CLARENDON

CENTER
RUTLAND

DAM

RUTLAND

DAM

US 4 US 7

DAM

PROCTOR
MARBLE MUSEUM

PITTSFORD

South Wallingford to Wallingford *(5¾ miles).*
The bridge at South Wallingford is a poor place to start, as the ledges extend under the bridge. Instead start at the bridge 1½ miles north, or anywhere the river approaches the road. The US 7 bridge (Mi. 4) is high and on a long causeway, but there is unlimited easy access from the gravel road on the west bank all the way to Wallingford.

Three bridges span the river in Wallingford. Between the VT 140 bridge, which is first, and the River Road bridge, which is last, are some riffles and an old canal on the right, best seen from the Mill Street bridge. The lefthand span of the last bridge is blocked by a ledge.

Typical farm scene along Otter Creek.

Wallingford to Rutland *(16 miles)*.

If you want an easier trip, you may put in below the third bridge in Wallingford. From here Otter Creek flows through valley farmland between steep, muddy banks. In 3½ miles, Mill River, which cuts through the main ridge of the Green Mountains at Clarendon Gorge, enters on the right. A small, shallow, sandy-bottomed pool has formed where the two rivers meet and makes a delightful spot for splashing around and getting wet on a warm day. Unless you are a very determined through-tripper, take out at the first Rutland bridge (Mi. 21¼), the fourth bridge below Wallingford, and portage by car past the Center Rutland dam.

Rutland to Center Rutland *(1¼ miles)*.

A quarter mile below the first Rutland bridge, the river passes over a low dam, visible from the road on the west bank. Although low, it is high enough to be dangerous but hard to see from the river, and people have washed over it by mistake. A rapid continues for ½ mile below with a bridge crossing overhead. The high dam at Center Rutland lies ½ mile below the rapid. Take out at the high double bridge, but expect a difficult climb up high, steep banks covered with small trees. The ½-mile carry can be made on either side; neither is particularly good, but the left is probably better. Carry down the railroad tracks through the factory yard, and then back to the river to the short rapid just below the dam (Mi. 22½). Those carrying by car can put in on either bank from side roads.

Center Rutland to Proctor *(7 miles)*.

After a little fast water below the high dam and rapid, the river runs flat for 7 miles to Proctor (Mi. 35½), flowing past wooded banks and farmland. At Proctor, take out on the right at the bridge to portage around the dam. Carry down the road on the right bank, turn left partway down the hill, and turn left again to the sewage treatment plant and onto the clay road. This road, which leads to the river, is drivable in dry weather. In wet weather, the cascade below the dam is lovely, but in dry weather all the water is diverted into the factory.

The large building on the left bank is the Marble Museum whose exhibits are open to the public (fee charged).

Proctor to Middlebury *(38 miles)*.

Otter Creek from Proctor to Middlebury is a popular canoe run through rural Vermont countryside with occasional fine views of the Green Mountains to the right. The current is slow and free of difficulties, while frequent bridges offer easy access. This stretch of the river should appeal to covered bridge lovers; six of these wooden structures still carry local traffic.

This long, unobstructed run ends at a dam in the college town of Middlebury (Mi. 67½). Five dams between this take-out and the mouth of the Lemon Fair require carries. Those who carry from here

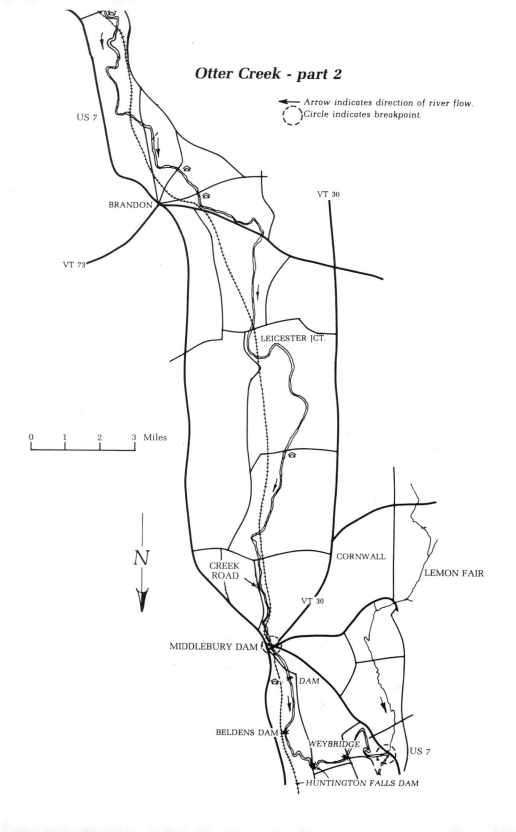

Otter Creek - part 2

← Arrow indicates direction of river flow.
◯ Circle indicates breakpoint.

US 7

VT 30

BRANDON

VT 73

LEICESTER JCT.

0   1   2   3 Miles

N

CREEK
ROAD

CORNWALL

LEMON FAIR

VT 30

MIDDLEBURY DAM

DAM

BELDENS DAM

WEYBRIDGE

US 7

HUNTINGTON FALLS DAM

by car will find a safe and convenient water level take-out 1½ miles above the town on the right. To reach the side road to this landing, drive south on US 7 from Middlebury and turn right onto Creek Road.

Middlebury to Lemon Fair *(12¼ miles)*.

Through-trippers who hand carry the dam at Middlebury should take out on the left as soon as they see the Middlebury bridge (or even before), as the dam is immediately below it. Carry up the bank, across the highway, and through a parking lot back down the river. Those carrying from here by car can load in the reserved parking lot on the left bank. Inspect the take-out by the dam in advance since the current picks up above the bridge.

This stretch of Otter Creek contains four more dams in addition to the one at Middlebury and generally appeals only to portaging enthusiasts. All but the second dam, at Beldens, are below bridges and should be portaged on the left.

To run lower Otter Creek, you can put in a Weybridge (Mi. 75½) either from the center of the island below the dam (which is not particularly easy) or from the right bank further downstream. The river is predominately quickwater from the dam to the mouth of the Lemon Fair (Mi. 79¾). (See Lemon Fair River—Otter Creek trip).

Canoeing beneath a covered bridge.

8   Lemon Fair—Otter Creek

Miles	Cumulative Miles	Break Points	River Rating	Special Difficulties
	0	**Lemon Fair River** West Cornwall		
11¾			Q	
	11¾	Otter Creek		
		Otter Creek Lemon Fair		
9			F,Q	Dam*
	20¾	Vergennes		
9			F,Q	
	29¾	Lake Champlain		

*Does not require portage if taking out at break point.

A trip down the Lemon Fair combines well with one on lower Otter Creek. Rising west of Brandon, the Lemon Fair flows parallel to and just west of Otter Creek and joins it about 4 miles below the Weybridge dam. The water is generally uninviting for swimmers, but the river is a real delight to the nature lover. Don't let the muddy water discourage you; it is caused by the clay bottom and, oddly enough, is muddier in low water than in high. (On most rivers, waters are clearer in low water than in high, because the slower currents cause the sandier sediment to settle out.) Although people may consider the water undesirable, birds, animals, and fish thrive on it. A steady plop-plopping of startled muskrats, turtles, and fish can be heard as the canoe approaches, and huge clouds of birds rise in advance. In fact, the whole river seems more like the Everglades than like Vermont. Many trees lining the banks have multiple trunks and intricate exposed root systems, and their branches sweep down over the river in a manner reminiscent of Florida's cypress and mangrove. If a submerged log were suddenly to open wide its jaws, it wouldn't seem a bit surprising.

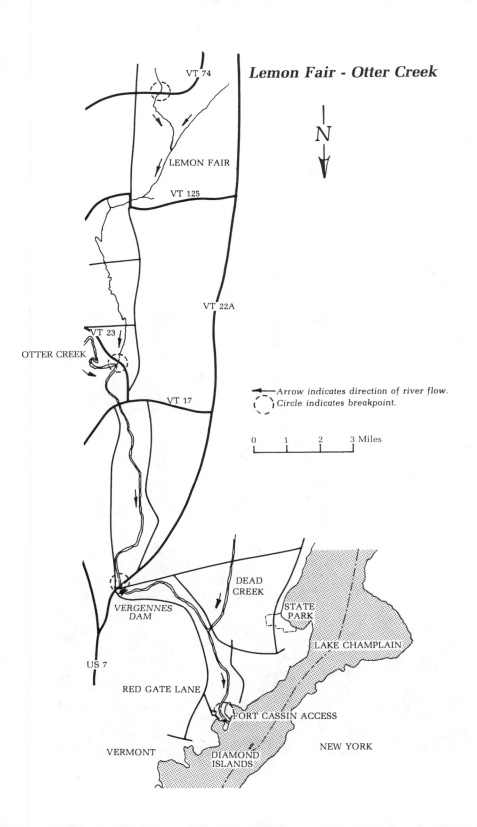

Lemon Fair - Otter Creek

VT 74

N

LEMON FAIR

VT 125

VT 22A

VT 23

OTTER CREEK

VT 17

Arrow indicates direction of river flow.
Circle indicates breakpoint.

0   1   2   3 Miles

DEAD
CREEK

STATE
PARK

LAKE CHAMPLAIN

VERGENNES
DAM

US 7

RED GATE LANE

FORT CASSIN ACCESS

NEW YORK

VERMONT   DIAMOND
ISLANDS

LEMON FAIR
West Cornwall to Otter Creek *(11¾ miles).*

Put in from the VT 74 bridge west of West Cornwall, or in low water from the VT 125 bridge (Mi. 4¾) further downstream. The Lemon Fair winds across low-lying fields drained by canals and is somewhat obstructed by water plants and fallen trees, particularly above VT 125. Flocks of heron congregate to feed in an especially marshy stretch between two side-road bridges which cross the lower portion. You reach higher ground shortly before the VT 23 bridge and the confluence of the Lemon Fair with Otter Creek (Mi. 11¾).

Reflections on the Lemon Fair.

OTTER CREEK

Lemon Fair River to Vergennes *(9 miles)*.

A marble monument stands high on the left bank of Otter Creek 0.1 mile upstream from the mouth of the Lemon Fair. Eight feet tall and surrounded by an iron fence, it is set in a horse pasture between road and river and is visible from both. The monument commemorates a raid in which Indians and Tories attacked a small settlement, burned the buildings, and carried the men and older boys off to Quebec. The women and children left behind hid in a cellar for ten days until they were rescued.

Otter Creek flows slowly and smoothly past farms and cornfields to Vergennes (Mi. 20¾). A trailer park and houses appear on the right bank ½ mile above the bridge; the dam at Vergennes lies just below the bridge and should be scouted in advance, if possible. The best landing, on the right just above the bridge, is close to the dam, and the current increases just as you reach it. Do not attempt this take-out if you are inexperienced or the river is high. The bank above this landing is overgrown and offers poor scouting or portaging. From your chosen landing above the bridge, carry along the road to the right up a steep hill. Watch for trucks barreling down the incline. Turn left onto MacDonough Drive and carry for 0.1 mile to a public landing.

On this site during the War of 1812, the MacDonough shipyard constructed gunboats for use on Lake Champlain and also built the ship *Saratoga* in only forty days. This small fleet spent the winter of 1813 at Buttonwoods, just above the mouth of Dead Creek. Because they feared the British would attempt to block Otter Creek's mouth, the Americans made a dugway to Lake Champlain from the left bank of Dead Creek, but it was never used.

Vergennes to Lake Champlain *(9 miles)*.

Below the dam at Vergennes, the river is deep and slow-moving, and you begin to see a few motorboats. In 4¾ miles, Dead Creek enters on the left. You can paddle up this marshy stream in a state-operated wildlife refuge; this makes a fine side trip for avid bird watchers. In high water the low bridge over the mouth of Dead Creek may not clear a canoe.

A short distance beyond Dead Creek are a few cottages, and the shores are posted against trespassing and fishing. Further downstream, the banks become swampy and continue so to Lake Champlain (Mi. 29¾).

The recommended take-out, the Fort Cassin fishing access and launching ramp, is located on the right off Red Gate Road ½ mile from the mouth of Otter Creek.

Nothing remains of Fort Cassin, a former gun emplacement, but its foundations, and a private cottage now occupies the site. The river's current here is negligible.

Lake Champlain presently has no public campsites in the immediate vicinity of Otter Creek. Button Bay State Park is 6 miles to the south. For swimming, a sandy town beach is tucked deep in a cove between Otter and Little Otter Creeks.

Lake Champlain.

This part of Lake Champlain is spectacular. If the weather permits, paddle north along the shore. The ledgy rock formations rise vertically from the water's edge and in places even overhang the lake, so that you can paddle directly under a cliff.

Along the Diamond Island cliffs.

The lake at this point is nearly 2 miles wide, and if the weather is good, you can venture across to the New York state shore. Remember though that large boats ply this lake and kick up a considerable wake. The Diamond Islands, minuscule rocky outcroppings, lie halfway across and just north of the mouth of Otter Creek. A white lighthouse marks the southernmost island.

The rock formations along the New York shore are quite different from those on the Vermont side. Split Rock Mountain rises steeply for hundreds of feet, and the area is uninhabited for miles in either direction. The steep, rocky shore makes it difficult to land and pull out a canoe in a heavy wind, and precious few places are even flat enough to sit on! This would be a poor place to get caught in a storm.

The views across the lake, however, are breath-taking. The Green Mountains with Mount Mansfield and the Camel's Hump rise in the distance to the east and the high peaks of the Adirondacks to the west. Take along a good map to help identify them.

9 Winooski River

Miles	Cumulative Miles	Break Points	River Rating	Special Difficulties
	0	Montpelier		
5½			Q,1	Rapids, Dam*
	5½	Middlesex		
10			F,Q,1,2	Waterfall*
	15½	Bolton Gorge		
23¾			F,Q,1	Dam*
	39¾	Essex Junction		
4¼			F,Q	
	43½	Essex		
4			X	recommend portage 2 dams and gorge
	47½	Winooski		
10			F,Q	
	57½	Lake Champlain		

*Does not require portage if taking out at break point.

The Winooski is the most spectacular of the three big rivers that cut through the Green Mountain Range. It rises in Vermont's eastern hills to flow westward past the state Capitol in Montpelier and empties into Lake Champlain just north of Burlington. Except where it slices through its renowned, deep-walled gorges, the river flows smoothly across the valley farmlands and the more expansive and fertile plains above Lake Champlain.

Although the upper Winooski has some pleasant, short runs, several dams make that portion unsuitable for a lengthy canoe camping trip. Dams are less frequent below Montpelier, where the Winooski can be run throughout the summer, although in very dry years there may be some shallow spots.

The Winooksi Valley Park Authority (Van Patten Parkway, Burlington, VT 05401) has been working on a "Canoe Trail" on the

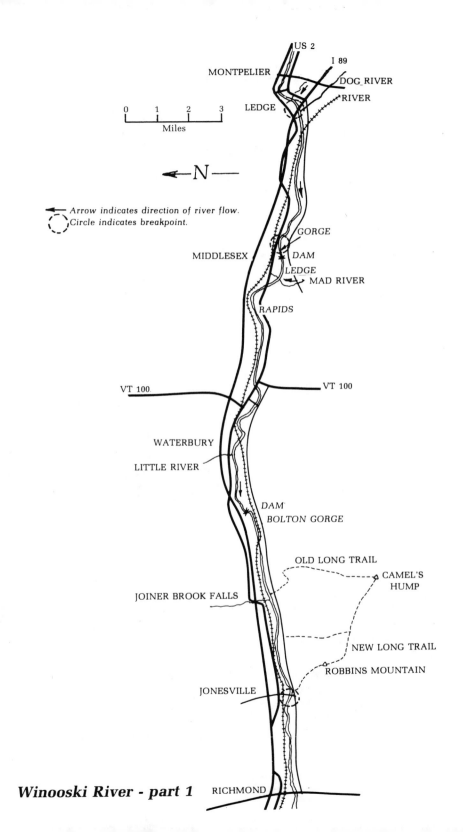

US 2

I 89

MONTPELIER

DOG RIVER

RIVER

LEDGE

0 1 2 3
Miles

←N—

←— Arrow indicates direction of river flow.
Circle indicates breakpoint.

GORGE

MIDDLESEX

DAM

LEDGE

MAD RIVER

RAPIDS

VT 100

VT 100

WATERBURY

LITTLE RIVER

DAM

BOLTON GORGE

OLD LONG TRAIL

CAMEL'S
HUMP

JOINER BROOK FALLS

NEW LONG TRAIL

ROBBINS MOUNTAIN

JONESVILLE

Winooski River - part 1   RICHMOND

Winooski and has signed some portages. The campsites are a location where it is permitted to camp and offer no amenities, sometimes not even a sign.

Montpelier to Middlesex *(5½ miles).*
Below Montpelier put in from the right bank from US 2 underneath the high interstate bridge. The Dog River enters on the left. The run to Middlesex Gorge is pleasant with occasional riffles and one ledge probably best run on the right.

Below the Middlesex bridge (Mi. 5½), keep to the left channel around the island and land on the left above the dam for a short carry.

Middlesex to Bolton Falls *(10 miles).*
The river valley begins to narrow at Middlesex, and beyond the dam the Winooski passes through a small gorge with sizable waves which you can see in the distance from the put-in below the dam. The gorge offers no special difficulties other than the high waves, and slack water below provides an opportunity to empty the canoe of excess water.

The Mad River empties into the Winooski about ½ mile further downstream (Mi. 6¼). There is a good swimming hole at the foot of the ledges ¼ mile upstream on the Mad River.

A class 2 ledge (more difficult in high water) lies around the corner downstream of the US 2 bridge (Mi. 6¾). High cliffs rise on one or both sides of the river with diminishing rapids for some distance downstream. At the far end a couple of old rings from logging days can be found in rocks in the center and on the left shore. From Waterbury to Bolton Falls the river flows peacefully across the narrow river valley. You pass beneath another US 2 bridge (Mi. 10¼), the first of three bridges in Waterbury, and 3 miles below town you come to the mouth of Little River (Mi. 13¼), which drains Waterbury Reservoir to the right.

After another 2 miles or so, the river swings north and starts to drop through the magnificent Bolton Gorge (Mi. 15½). Here the Winooski breaks through the Green Mountains' main ridge (the Camel's Hump stands out boldly on the left) and cuts deeply through high rock cliffs to plunge over Bolton Falls. Strong current makes the approach very dangerous.

Take out on the left bank at the southern swing where the river starts to bend toward the gorge. You can just barely see the gorge here to the right, rapids lie ahead, and a power line runs across a hilltop. Carry across the field, along the railroad track or the dirt road beyond. The dam has been rebuilt, and a good road leads down to a picnic area and boat launching. The total portage is ¾ mile.

A short hike up the side road from the pool to the top of the cliff under the power line allows a tremendous view of the gorge and of Camel's Hump in the distance. For a different vantage point, walk up another side road from the pool to the old powerhouse foundations at the foot of the old dam. The gorge is also visible from the east-bound lane of I-89 just before the rest area (but not from the west-bound lane or from US 2).

Bolton Falls to Essex Junction *(23¾ miles)*.

A campsite is on the right half a mile downstream.

Less than a mile beyond Bolton Gorge you reach a railroad bridge supported by four pilings (Mi. 16¼). The five channels around them are sprinkled with rocks which cause trouble in low water while the pilings themselves present problems in high water. From here to Jonesville, the river is predominantly slow current.

The Long Trail used to come down the Banforth Ridge (Mi. 18¾). At that time it met the Winooski 2½ miles below the railroad bridge. There is no bridge here, and the older trail guides recommended that hikers hail the farmer on the far bank who would ferry people across in his rowboat. Those with insufficient lungpower to raise an otherwise occupied farmer were directed upstream to the railroad bridge or downstream to Jonesville.

After crossing the river, the old trail continued north along Joiner Brook past a fascinating waterfall with interesting potholes and a swimming hole (just above US 2), and then followed the brook along a logging trail.

Because the crossing was difficult and also because the logging road was paved and now leads to a ski area, the trail was relocated west to cross the Winooski over the Jonesville bridge (Mi. 22¼). With an elevation of only 326 feet, this is the Long Trail's lowest point. For a panoramic view over the Winooski Valley to Lake Champlain, follow the trail for 2 miles south and a 1700-foot climb to the beacon on Robbins Mountain.

The river flows smoothly with gradually diminishing current for the next 17 miles to Essex Junction. Camel's Hump can be seen to the southeast and Mount Mansfield stands out boldly to the northeast. The Winooski Valley opens up beyond the Richmond bridge (Mi. 25½), and the river meanders back and forth across the broad plain. The I-89 and US 2 bridges cross together about 3 miles below Richmond (Mi. 28½). Another 5¼ miles brings you to the North Williston bridge (Mi. 33¾). The power dam at Essex Junction (Mi. 39¼) lies 5½ miles further downstream.

The portage on the left starts near the sharp turn at the dam, follows down past the power station and across the road to Overlook Park, furnished by the Green Mountain Power Company, with tables, grills and outhouses. (This is not the "campsite," which is on the river well upstream of the dam on the left on the property of Morris Brown.) From the picnic area the trail slabs the steep rocks to the river.

The footing is better, and a car can be used, if you take out on the right on the private road to IBM, cross the highway and turn left, then right on Cascade Road, and down a dirt track to the river. Beware of traffic in either case.

Winooski River - part 2

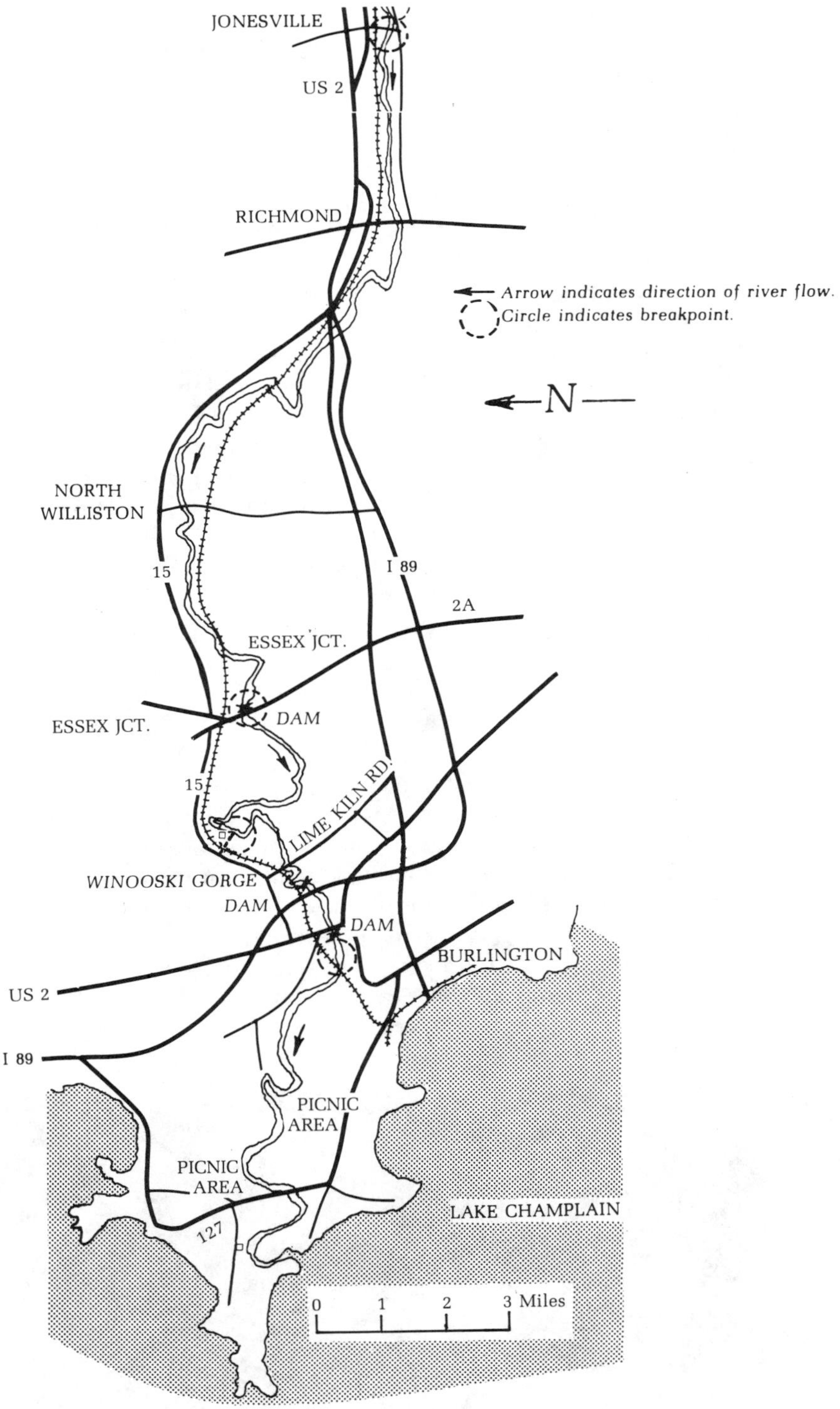

JONESVILLE

US 2

RICHMOND

Arrow indicates direction of river flow.
Circle indicates breakpoint.

←N—

NORTH
WILLISTON

15

I 89

2A

ESSEX JCT.

ESSEX JCT.   DAM

15

LIME KILN RD.

WINOOSKI GORGE
DAM

DAM

BURLINGTON

US 2

I 89

PICNIC
AREA

PICNIC
AREA

LAKE CHAMPLAIN

127

| 0 | 1 | 2 | 3 Miles |

Essex Junction to Essex *(4¼ miles).*

Class 1 water extends about ½ mile below the power dam. The river twists for another 4 miles of slowish water before the current begins to pick up leading into Winooski Gorge. The best way to handle the gorge is to take out at the old military reservation, where there is a ramp, and carry by car.

By car this ramp is ½ mile east of the Fanny Allen Hospital on VT 15, the southern extention at a crossroad with a small sign "Town of Essex recreation land." Follow down it to the river.

Essex to Winooski *(4 miles).*

It is possible to paddle to the sewage treatment plant another mile downstream on the right and take out there. There is no access at Lime Kiln Road, which provides a scenic view of the sheer cliffs which it crosses. A dam lies in the next gorge ½ mile downstream of this bridge, which is not feasible to carry at that point. Rapids continue under the interstate bridge, with cascades above the dam in Winooski. An additional hazard is that what you see is not necessarily what you get: the water level is controlled by the dam at Essex Junction, so it can rise suddenly, greatly increasing the force of the current.

Winooski to Lake Champlain *(10 miles).*

From the previous take-out, continue west on the highway to the road which crosses the bridge in Winooski. Turn left, then right on West Canal Street, on the north side of the river. Put in behind one of the old mill buildings.

The railroad recrosses the river ½ mile below. The river starts a series of wide meanders around the edge of Burlington. The Winooski Valley Park Authority has established a picnic area 4 miles downstream on the left near their headquarters at the end of Van Patten Parkway, and another further down on the right. The VT 127 bridge crosses at Mi. 55¾. The recommended take-out is a fishing access further downstream on the right side just above the river's mouth at Lake Champlain (Mi. 58½).

Ring in mid-river rock used to anchor log boom.

10   *Lamoille River*

Miles	Cumulative Miles	Break Points	River Rating	Special Difficulties
	0	Johnson		
12¾			Q,1	2 ledges (class 2-3)
	12½	Jeffersonville		
14½			Q	Dam*
	27¼	Fairfax Falls		
6½			1,2,3	
	33¼	Arrowhead Mountain Lake		
3¾			F	Dam*
	37	Milton Dam		
3¾			F,1	Dam*
	40¾	West Milton Dam		
5¾			F	
	46½	Lake Champlain		

*Does not require portage if taking out at break point.

One of three big rivers that breaks through the main ridge of the Green Mountains, the Lamoille flows west across northern Vermont to enter Lake Champlain above Burlington. In its course, it passes through the second deepest trench in the Green Mountain range and then wends its way across typical Vermont countryside. The Lamoille Valley is wider than that of the Winooski and its towns are smaller. The upper portion, where the river flows easily and quickly, is better for canoe camping as the shorter flatwater stretches below Fairfax Falls are broken by two dams and rapids which require portages. Mountain views to both sides are excellent, and one of Vermont's two remaining covered railroad bridges spans the river east of Johnson, although not on the portion described here.

Lamoille River - part 1

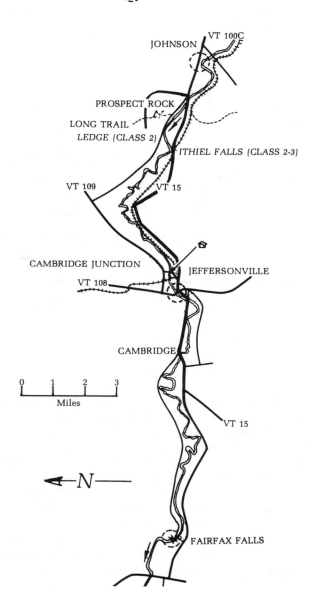

Arrow indicates direction of river flow.
Circle indicates breakpoint.

VT 100C

JOHNSON

PROSPECT ROCK

LONG TRAIL
LEDGE (CLASS 2)

ITHIEL FALLS (CLASS 2-3)

VT 109   VT 15

CAMBRIDGE JUNCTION

JEFFERSONVILLE

VT 108

CAMBRIDGE

0   1   2   3
Miles

VT 15

←N—

FAIRFAX FALLS

Johnson to Jeffersonville *(12¾ miles).*
Put in off VT 15 above the Johnson bridge. The river runs placidly for a short 2¼ miles to the VT 15 bridge below the town.

The Long Trail crosses the Lamoille at the VT 15 bridge. With an elevation of only 500 feet, this is the trail's second lowest point. For an excellent view of the Lamoille Valley, follow the Long Trail north (downstream) along the dirt road high on the right bank for about 1 mile, and then climb steeply for ¾ mile to Prospect Rock. You can see the Sterling Range to the south, but nearby peaks obscure Mount Mansfield 10 miles southwest. The road up the notch behind Prospect Rock is now drivable so you may prefer to drive up while doing your car shuttle.

Note difference in freeboard between 2 styles of canoe.

Shortly after passing the VT 15 bridge you reach a ledge with a 100-yard, class 2 rapid which is rocky in low water and has standing waves in high water. A mile further on, Ithiel Falls is similar but somewhat more difficult, especially in high water. The first ledge is visible from the dirt road on the right, but Ithiel Falls cannot be conveniently scouted in advance.

Where the river comes close to the road again on the right bank, it divides to flow swiftly around several large granite islands; if you wish to avoid the ledges, put in here (Mi. 3¾). Below this short stretch of fast water, the Lamoille begins its leisurely meander across the valley floor.

A side road crosses the river on a covered bridge at Cambridge Junction (Mi. 11), and VT 108 crosses at Jeffersonville (Mi. 12¼), with best access upstream on right at rest area.

Jeffersonville to Fairfax Falls *(14½ miles).*
Below the VT 15 bridge (Mi. 12¾), the river continues to meander through pastoral countryside to Fairfax Falls; Mount Mansfield, Vermont's highest peak, is clearly visible to the southeast. At Cambridge (Mi. 15¾), VT 15 again crosses the river.

To portage the dam at Fairfax Falls, take out on the left at the bridge (Mi. 26½) and carry down the road ¼ mile to the power station (Mi. 26¾).

Fairfax Falls to Arrowhead Mountain Lake *(6½ miles).*
Below the dam, fast water continues for 2 miles to the VT 104 bridge at Fairfax (Mi. 28¾). The short stretch of easy rapids below is followed by about 1 mile of flattish water. Around a bend in the river to the left, you begin to hear and then see the whitecaps of Two Islands Rapids. In medium water, these rapids are class 2 to 3 and should be inspected before they are run. Fast water and easy rapids extend for another 2 miles to Five Chutes. These chutes are formed by a transverse ledge and are class 2 in medium water. Each of them can be run, and canoe groups frequently spend a long time here trying them all. Of all the rapids along this stretch only Five Chutes can be scouted in advance; take a dirt road on the left bank, which is approached from the East Georgia bridge.

It is ¼ mile from Five Chutes to the bridge at East Georgia and just beyond it lies Arrowhead Mountain Lake (Mi. 33¼).

Arrowhead Mountain Lake to Milton Dam *(3¾ miles).*
Arrowhead Mountain Lake, formed by the Milton Dam, is shaped like a backward question mark. Put in or take out at a fishing access on the lake's north end. A relatively small lake, its wider upper end is dotted with islands while the lower, southern end reaches into a narrow valley and is not much wider than the original river. Take out on either side above the dam (Mi. 37).

Lamoille River - part 2

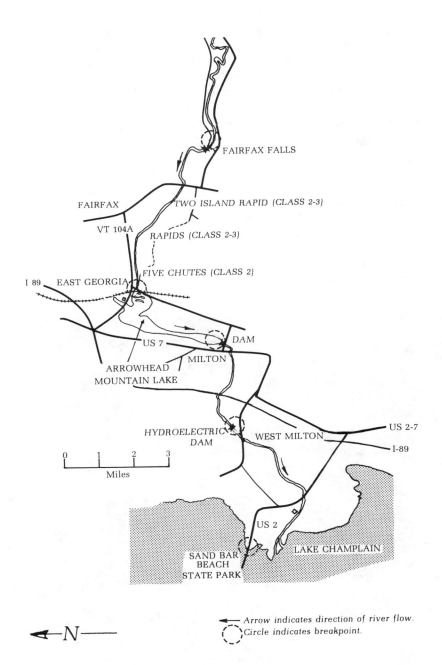

FAIRFAX FALLS

TWO ISLAND RAPID (CLASS 2-3)

FAIRFAX

VT 104A

RAPIDS (CLASS 2-3)

FIVE CHUTES (CLASS 2)

I 89   EAST GEORGIA

US 7

ARROWHEAD
MOUNTAIN LAKE

DAM

MILTON

HYDROELECTRIC
DAM

WEST MILTON

US 2-7

I-89

US 2

SAND BAR
BEACH
STATE PARK

LAKE CHAMPLAIN

0   1   2   3

Miles

←N—

Arrow indicates direction of river flow.
Circle indicates breakpoint.

Milton Dam to West Milton Dam *(3¾ miles).*

From Arrowhead Mountain Lake, portage along the road for about 1 mile to the Milton Hydroelectric Station.

After 1 mile of fast water, you pass under I-89 and enter the backwater from the Peterson Hydroelectric Dam at West Milton. The remaining 1¾ miles to this dam are very wild and scenic. Be careful when approaching the dam (Mi. 40¾); take out on the left bank past the last large ledge outcrop to portage. Carry along the power station access road as far as the town road, unless you want to run the 100 yards of class 3 rapids immediately below the dam.

West Milton Dam to Lake Champlain *(5¾ miles).*

The Lamoille has flatwater for its last 5½ miles to Lake Champlain. The West Milton bridge crosses ½ mile below the dam, and the Adirondacks across Lake Champlain are visible in the distance ahead. About 3 miles further downstream, you pass under US 2 (Mi. 44¼); the last access on the river is a short distance beyond. The mouth of the Lamoille is marshy, and the main channel meanders through a fair-sized delta.

Sand Bar Beach State Park on the lake lies 1½ miles north of the river and is a pleasant place to end your trip.

If the fish aren't biting, you can pan for gold. If all else fails, bake biscuits in the pan.

11 Missisquoi River

Miles	Cumulative Miles	Break Points	River Rating	Special Difficulties
	0	North Troy		
16			F,Q	
	16	East Richford		
18½			F,Q,1	2 rapids (class 2-3) Dam washing out Dam*
	34½	Enosburg Falls		
11			F,Q,2	Dam*
	45½	Sheldon Springs		
8¼			F,Q,2	"Unrunnable" ledge Dam*
	53¾	Highgate Falls		
7			F,Q	Dam*
	60¾	Swanton		
8			F,Q	
	68¾	Lake Champlain		

*Does not require portage if taking out at break point.

One of Vermont's northern-most rivers, the Missisquoi runs north along the eastern slopes of the Green Mountains into Quebec where it loops through the range's northern foothills. Crossing back into Vermont, it flows west to drain into Missisquoi Bay at the northern end of Lake Champlain. The river passes only small towns, and most local mills no longer discharge wastes into the river, so its waters are fairly clean.

Downstream from North Troy, the river alternates between fast current and smooth flatwater broken by occasional rapids and dams. Only four of the largest dams once built below North Troy remain intact. These do not affect canoeing, since natural waterfalls at these sites would have to be portaged anyway.

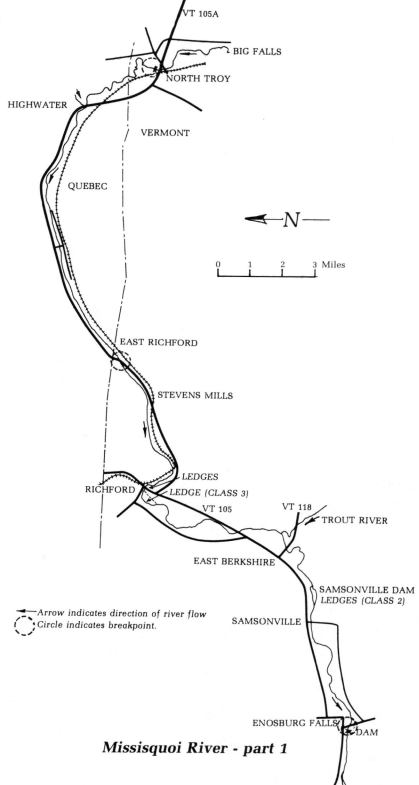

Missisquoi River - part 1

Just before reaching North Troy, the Missisquoi passes through Big Falls, a splendid gorge which merits a side trip. To see it, drive 2 miles south from North Troy on River Road along the east bank. The river undercuts a fifty-foot cliff, and the upper cacades ¼ mile above the falls have some interesting eroded ledges and potholes.

North Troy to East Richford *(16 miles)*.
North Troy is just south of the Canadian border on VT 105. Before unloading, drive 1½ miles north on VT 105A and report to Canadian Customs.

Metal flange protects bird nest from predators.

The hardest part of the stretch is putting in *below* the North Troy dam. A devious route through the millyard and across the railroad tracks goes along the right bank to the river. You can also put in from a farm off Pine Street on the right bank, 1 mile further downstream. This spot is better in dry weather, since you must negotiate a dirt track ½ mile long before you reach the river.

Beware when asking directions to a good put-in; some townsfolk think "below the dam" means to the south, and may direct you to the nice landing off River Road which unfortunately is *upstream* of the dam.

Across the border in Quebec, the Missisquoi seems not to cut through the mountains but to outflank them. Below Highwater (Mi. 5¾) in Quebec, the river meanders through a fairly broad valley with farmland broken by patches of woodland. Shortly after the first bridge a campground (Mi. 6) fronts the river on the right. A side road crosses in another 5 miles or so where the Missisquoi curves southwest and flows back into Vermont.

Heed the sign at the high bridge in East Richford (Mi. 16) and land upstream on the left to report to American Customs just at the top of the bank.

East Richford to Enosburg Falls *(18½ miles)*.
The first 5 miles from East Richford to Richford (Mi. 21) are predominantly class 1 water. Numerous islands create networks of channels and intricate bifurcations; the banks are very wild and scenic, but careful water reading is necessary to pick out the best channels.

For the length of the Richford rapids, the river is contained within sheer bridge abutments and high retaining walls and is impeded with transverse ledges; since the rapids are easily seen from the Richford bridge, it is best to scout them in advance to plan a course of action. Just downstream of the bridge a river-level gauge is painted on a building on the left; we found 1½ feet a good height to run the river.

Watch for a railroad bridge crossing the Missisquoi 1¼ miles above Richford. Shortly afterward, the river comes close to the road; this is a possible take-out if you do not wish to run the rapids that start just below a factory on the left bank. The class 2 ledges above the Richford bridge should be run well on the left. The rapids continue below the bridge, increase in intensity, and culminate in a big drop over a class 3 ledge. A clear but narrow channel runs down to the left of center through large standing waves.

The river divides around a small island below the town. An old USGS topographic map shows the main channel to the left, but a dam now shunts the river to the right.

Slower current, occasional riffles, some flatwater, and impressive mountain views characterize the run below Richford to Samsonville (Mi. 30). To the left rise the Green Mountains' northern peaks and to

Missisquoi River - part 2

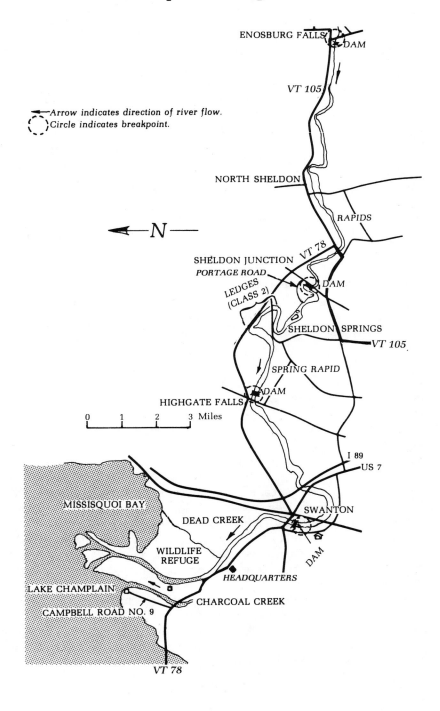

ENOSBURG FALLS DAM

VT 105

Arrow indicates direction of river flow.
Circle indicates breakpoint.

NORTH SHELDON

RAPIDS

←—N—

SHELDON JUNCTION VT 78
PORTAGE ROAD
LEDGES
(CLASS 2) DAM

SHELDON SPRINGS
VT 105

SPRING RAPID

DAM
HIGHGATE FALLS

0   1   2   3 Miles

I 89
US 7

MISSISQUOI BAY

DEAD CREEK

SWANTON

WILDLIFE
REFUGE

DAM

HEADQUARTERS

LAKE CHAMPLAIN

CHARCOAL CREEK

CAMPBELL ROAD NO. 9

VT 78

the right the lower more rounded hills along the international border.

The railroad and VT 105 bridges (Mi. 25¾) cross together 5 miles below Richford. Trout River enters on the left 1½ miles downstream, and ½ mile below, VT 118 crosses at East Berkshire (Mi. 27¾).

Parts of the old Samsonville dam (Mi. 29¾) still stand in the middle of the river 2 miles below the VT 118 bridge. You can see the dam and the ledges below it from VT 105. The dam is now breached on the left as well as the right. Most people find it easiest to portage or line on the left. Only those who thought the Richford drop was easy should land on the right to look this ledge over before running it. It has a considerable backroller and should be scouted carefully; spikes have caused problems in low water. Since the dam is washing out, conditions will change after each storm. Class 2 ledges immediately below continue for about ½ mile and can be run in several places.

A little over 1 mile below the Samsonville dam, you pass under the North Enosburg bridge (Mi. 31); smooth water continues to Enosburg Falls (Mi. 34½). Land above the bridge to portage the dam: on the right if you wish to run the rapids immediately below, or on the left to make the longer carry around them.

Enosburg Falls to Sheldon Springs *(11 miles).*

The water remains smooth for another 6 miles to the North Sheldon bridge (Mi. 40¾). The 3 miles of rapids between the bridges at North Sheldon and Sheldon Junction (Mi. 43¼) are scratchy or impossible in very low water. The river flows gently again for the remaining 2 miles to Sheldon Springs. Take out on the right above the bridge (Mi. 45⅛) to portage the dam below. No take-out is marked.

Sheldon Springs to Highgate Falls *(8¼ miles).*

An extensive cascade drops below the newly rebuilt dam. The access on the left is for heavy water enthusiasts with expert canoeing skill, who have scouted it carefully.

The portage to the foot of the rapids starts by turning right on the road. Take the second gate to the left in a tenth of a mile, which is marked by large Boise Cascade signs. Follow the paved road around and down a steep hill to the power station. Total portage 1.3 miles. Cars may be driven down this road to unload. Get permission before parking.

Water level in this and the subsequent section may fluctuate drastically when the gates are opened and closed for power generation. For information on scheduled discharges of water—and on parking—call Boise Cascade (802) 933-7733.

You can run the rapid's lower end if you wish. Below, the river continues for a pleasant 3-mile paddle. This stretch was seldom run in the past because the plywood and wood products mill at Sheldon Springs discharged effluent and bark chips here. The plant has cleaned up its operation, and no signs of earlier pollution remain.

A stretch of rapids and class 2 ledges begins just above the bridge in East Highgate (Mi. 49½); you may scout this in advance from either the bridge or VT 78 on the right bank. These ledges have shallow spots and sharp drops which require careful planning, and the abutments of an old dam, in the process of being undermined, still stand just below the bridge. The rapids continue for ½ mile, with their whole length visible from the road.

Below the rapids, the Missisquoi again leaves the highway. One mile above Highgate Falls, you begin to hear the river roar as it rushes through two ledges ¹⁄₁₀ mile apart. Unfortunately, you cannot conveniently scout these ledges in advance. Although the first can be run, the second drops 5 feet and is unrunnable over the main drop for all but the suicidal ledge enthusiast. However, a strong, skillful paddler can land on the right just above the second for an easy carry. Those who miss this landing will regret it. You may choose to begin your carry further upstream on the right. Those who line should work on the left where the drop is more even and the river more shallow. You can also line the main drop on the left.

This set of ledges is called "Spring Rapid," in reference to a mineral spring in the woods high to the left. Water from the spring was once bottled and sold for medicinal purposes.

Below the ledges the river broadens into a pond behind the dam at Highgate Falls (Mi. 53¾). The dam lies *above* an old iron bridge which replaced one of Vermont's earliest covered bridges and was recently designated a historical landmark. A new bridge is around the corner downstream. Take out on the left in the bay. Carry on the road across VT 207 and down to the power station.

Like many of Vermont's dams, the dam at Highgate Falls is one of a series that has occupied the site. The first dam at Highgate Falls was built in 1807 to drive a waterwheel, which generated power for a sawmill; after a few years of operation, it was washed downstream by spring ice and high water. The Keyes family, who at the time owned a good share of Highgate, rebuilt it to power a grist mill. A generating plant added later furnished the surrounding area with electrical power: this plant was eventually sold to the village of Swanton, which in turn built a new dam. Portions of the old wooden dam are still in place behind the present structure.

Highgate Falls to Swanton (7 miles).

Below the dam and around the bend, the river broadens into a large pool dotted with islands. Smooth water continues to Swanton (Mi. 61). Three bridges cross the Missisquoi on this stretch: the I-89 bridge (Mi. 57½), the US 7 bridge (Mi. 57¾), and an old covered railroad bridge (Mi. 60½). The latter, now abandoned, is one of only two covered railroad bridges still standing in Vermont. (The other, still in use, crosses the Lamoille east of Johnson.) Take out on either side above the Swanton dam which lies *above* the VT 78 bridge (Mi. 60¾).

Swanton to Lake Champlain *(8 miles)*.

Below Swanton the river is essentially lake travel. The first stretch runs parallel to VT 78, and backyards of several homes extend to the river bank. Dead Creek, a side stream of the Missisquoi delta, branches off from the river opposite the Missisquoi Wildlife Refuge Headquarters (Mi. 63¼). There is no access at the headquarters.

Dead Creek itself is attractive, and the area around it abounds in wildlife. Since fewer power boats use this channel, you may prefer this route to the lake. The water is shallow with much vegetation and lies further east than the map would imply. Paddle a short distance east across the bay to take out at the small resort town of Highgate Springs.

An alternate take-out is the boat-launching ramp (Mi. 64¼) on the Missisquoi 1 mile below the Dead Creek junction. The river below here is well traveled by motorboats going to or from Lake Champlain (Mi. 68¾).

A third possible take-out is a marina on the lake 1½ miles south-west (left) on the river mouth. It is situated on a point west of a blind channel called Charcoal Creek; you can reach it by car from Campbell Road 9, which follows Charcoal Creek.

Ledges below the bridge at Richford.

12 Connecticut River (West Stewartstown to Gilman)

Miles	Cumulative Miles	Break Points	River Rating	Special Difficulties
	0	West Stewartstown		
15			Q,1	
	15	Columbia		
9¼			Q,1,2	Old dam
	24½	North Stratford		
11¼			Q	
	35¾	Stratford		
12¾			F,Q	Old dam*
	48½	Guildhall, Vermont		
20½			F,Q,1	Dam*
	69	Gilman Dam		

*Does not require portage if taking out at break point.

The Connecticut River watershed forms the northern boundary between New Hampshire and Quebec, and further downstream the river itself divides Vermont and New Hampshire before crossing into Massachusetts. Since the state line is fixed at the low-water mark on the Vermont shore, the upper Connecticut is actually in New Hampshire and is that state's longest river.

A long river with a moderate current and easy rapids, the Connecticut is very popular for canoeing, despite the aura of civilization and occasional dams. The 69-mile stretch from West Stewartstown near Quebec to Gilman contains some of the faster water on the Connecticut, although the river is mostly smooth. Only one long stretch of rapids and one old dam require special attention.

The Connecticut's drainage basin covers extensive timberland. This long river was an obvious choice for transporting logs to lumber

Connecticut River - part 1

Arrow indicates direction of river flow.
Circle indicates breakpoint.

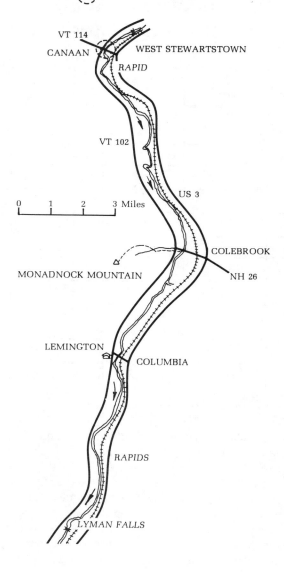

VT 114

CANAAN

WEST STEWARTSTOWN

RAPID

VT 102

US 3

0   1   2   3 Miles

COLEBROOK

MONADNOCK MOUNTAIN

NH 26

N

LEMINGTON

COLUMBIA

RAPIDS

LYMAN FALLS

mills further downstream, and log drives were once an annual event. Today, you can still find evidence of this earlier use along the river.

Before a log drive, cut logs were piled along the river banks in rollways. When the drive was ready to begin, the stakes holding these piles were removed—a very dangerous proceeding since on occasion the whole pile would suddenly collapse and flatten whatever or whomever was in the way. Since a successful drive required an exact amount of water, small dams which could be blown out easily were built on the tributaries.

The rivermen had to keep the logs moving. Crews and teams of horses along both shores followed waist-deep in icy water to push stranded logs back into the current. Occasionally rapids were blasted apart to release or prevent big jams, and loggers had a running feud with owners of small mill dams along the way.

Log booms (long lines of log chained together) also directed the floating timber. Strung across a blind eddy, they prevented swirling jams; fanned out above a dam, they guided the logs into a sluice; and stretched across a quiet part of the river by a mill, they brought the log drive to an end. Cables on trees or rings in the rock, some of which still remain, held the booms. When a needed natural anchorage did not exist a log crib was manufactured. A cube of heavy timbers was laid up log cabin style and filled with rocks and dirt to create an artificial island. These were built to withstand great pressure, and many still remain.

During the big log drives, everything from saw logs to huge cookrafts ran the river. Rivermen on saw logs could move from one log to another, paddling with a peavey or in shallow water poling with a pikepole. They could also move ahead by jumping violently down on one end, or sideways by rolling it.

The boat loggers favored was a bateau. Its narrow bottom enabled it to spin easily, and its long, raking overhang and flared sides helped it to slide over obstructions and float heavy loads in shallow water. Bateaux could run rocky rapids and heavy white water better than any other work boat and could be handled with oars, paddles, or poles.

A cookshack mounted on a huge raft often accompanied the crew and logs down the river. These cook rafts could run the dam at Guildhall and many big rapids, but at particularly high dams they had to be dismantled and reassembled below. (The large Comerford and Moore Dams, which innundated the Fifteen Mile Falls section of rapids downstream of the portion described here, were not built until after the last of the log drives.)

West Stewartstown to Columbia (15 miles).

The usual start for a trip on the upper Connecticut is the Vermont end of the Canaan-West Stewartstown bridge, off US 3 and near the junction of VT 102 and VT 114. The river here has few rocks and can usually be run even in very low water; dams upstream control the water level.

Just beyond the first corner to the left, the river divides around two long, thin islands into three channels of runnable rapids. A moderate current continues to Colebrook as the river passes through a beautiful valley with woods and low-lying farmland close to the banks. Roads follow along both sides, but not closely.

When the river circles around to the left, Vermont's Monadnock Mountain becomes conspicuous ahead on the right. A trail up the mountain starts near the Colebrook Bridge (Mi. 10¼).

To climb Monadnock, land on the right downstream from the bridge. From telephone pole #NETT 81 PSCO 14, go up a farm lane between two houses, crawl under the gate, continue through the horse pasture, and cross the brook. A woods road follows the right bank of this brook upstream and degenerates into a trail. In season, the wildflowers are beautiful. After 1 mile, the trail crosses to the left bank above a waterfall and then continues for another 1½ miles up through a forest of small evergreens to the summit, where an old fire tower offers a good view of the river valley and surrounding hills.

Replica of bateau owned by Dearborn Company of the New Hampshire Militia.

Connecticut River - part 2

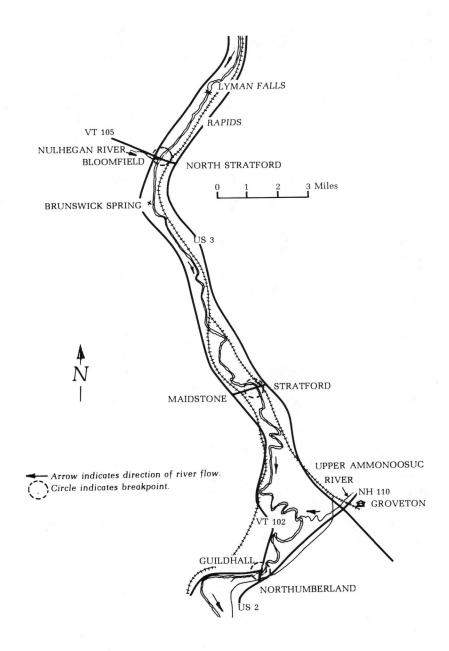

LYMAN FALLS

RAPIDS

VT 105

NULHEGAN RIVER
BLOOMFIELD

NORTH STRATFORD

0   1   2   3 Miles

BRUNSWICK SPRING

US 3

N

STRATFORD

MAIDSTONE

UPPER AMMONOOSUC
RIVER

NH 110

GROVETON

Arrow indicates direction of river flow.
Circle indicates breakpoint.

VT 102

GUILDHALL

NORTHUMBERLAND

US 2

Below Colebrook, smooth water alternates with easy rapids to the covered Columbia Bridge (Mi. 15).

Columbia to North Stratford *(9¼ miles).*

Below Columbia, the river continues to flow smoothly for about 2 more miles. It then enters a long stretch of class 2 rapids which continue intermittently over the next 7½ miles to the Bloomfield-North Stratford bridge. In low water, these rapids are too rocky to run. VT 102 comes close to the river where the rapids begin, so you can easily scout the first stretch in advance or take out if necessary.

About 5 miles from the onset of rapids, the old Lyman Falls Dam (Mi. 22) is exceedingly difficult to spot from above, and in high water canoes are frequently swept over it by mistake. As you round a gentle lefthand turn where the river is wide with a side channel cutting left and a steep bank on the right, watch for a log crib near the right bank. The dam lies just below it. Land on the Vermont side to scout, line, run, or carry. Even at suitable water levels, many people choose not to run this spot because of the spikes and jagged blocks which remain from the old dam. With difficulty, you can inspect the dam in advance from VT 102, ¼ mile downstream from the Vermont Highway Department garage.

Beyond the dam, the rapids become easier as you approach the Bloomfield North Stratford bridge (Mi. 24½).

North Stratford to Stratford *(11¼ miles).*

There are no rapids below North Stratford, and the river again runs smoothly for the next 11¼ miles. A rapid called the "Horserace" was mistakenly located here in some earlier guidebooks. Different sources place this rapid in different locations, but all the spots mentioned are now innundated by the backwater of the Comerford and Moore Dams and are all well downstream of Gilman, the final take-out on this portion of the Connecticut.

About 1½ miles from the North Stratford bridge and just upstream of a high cliff on the right, a distinctive brownish stain in the water marks the Brunswick Mineral Spring location (Mi. 26). An old hotel catering to those who came for the spring's mineral waters once stood above this spot.

Past the cliff, the river winds through farmland and pasture to the Maidstone-Stratford bridge (Mi. 35¾), above which you can take out on the right.

Stratford to Guildhall *(12¾ miles).*

The river continues to wander placidly down the valley to Guildhall, still uninterrupted by rapids. The Upper Ammonoosuc River (Mi. 45¾), which enters on the left 10 miles below Stratford, used to bring polluted water from the mills at Groveton. Now the water is treated, and this greatly improves the run downstream. You can see the Percy Peaks, a pair of sharp, pointed mountains in New

Lifting canoe past an old log dam.

Pouring tea.

Connecticut River - part 3

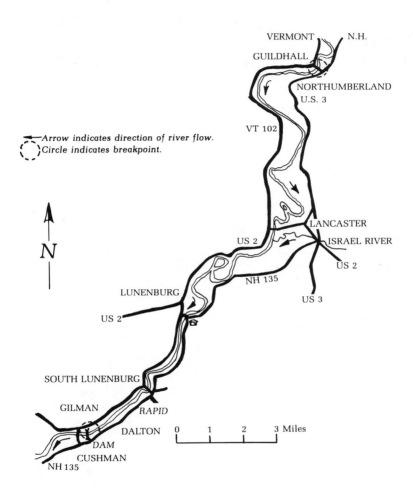

VERMONT   N.H.

GUILDHALL

NORTHUMBERLAND
U.S. 3

VT 102

Arrow indicates direction of river flow.
Circle indicates breakpoint.

LANCASTER

US 2   ISRAEL RIVER

US 2

N

NH 135

US 3

LUNENBURG

US 2

SOUTH LUNENBURG

GILMAN   RAPID

DALTON   0   1   2   3 Miles

DAM

CUSHMAN

NH 135

Hampshire, here on the left. About 3 miles further and just below the bridge is the old dam at Guildhall (Mi. 48½). Take out above the bridge on either side.

Guildhall to Gilman Dam *(20½ miles).*

The old dam at Guildhall is pretty well washed out. This section features some well preserved log cribs and other logging remains. The countryside is rural; the meanders are very deep, with attractive sandbars. The US 2 bridge is 9¼ miles downstream, and the covered bridge another 4¾. Below the RR bridge in South Lunenburg (Mi. 18) is a class 1 rapid with boulders in the middle and on the left. Keep right.

The portage trail at Gilman Dam starts in a deep bay on the left above the log boom, leading to a gravel road where a car may be driven.

13 Connecticut River (Comerford Dam to Orford)

Miles	Cumulative Miles	Break Points	River Rating	Special Difficulties
	0	Comerford Dam		
6¾			Q,1	Dam*
	6¾	McIndoe Falls		
8¼			F,Q,1,2	Dam
	15	Woodsville		
10½			Q	
	25½	Newbury		
18			F	
	43½	Orford		

*Does not require portage if taking out at break point.

The Connecticut River from Comerford Dam, west of Littleton, New Hampshire, to Orford is fairly large and can be run anytime, although occasional shallow spots may appear in the wider expanses. The river is mostly quickwater along this 43-mile stretch, with a few riffles and easy rapids and two large dams which require portages. The stretch from Newbury to Wilder Dam, 20 miles below Orford, is especially popular with several campgrounds, picnic areas, and launching ramps between Orford and Wilder Dam. Current information on water flow and campsites in this area is available at the Visitors Information Center at either Moore Dam (upstream of Comerford Dam) or Wilder Dam (below Hanover). Both centers are in New Hampshire.

Comerford Dam to McIndoe Falls (6¾ miles).
Comerford Dam can only be reached from the New Hampshire side of the river off NH 135; unfortunately, access below the dam is rather tedious. Carry down the grassy slope adjacent to the dam, slide down a steep, rocky incline, and continue downstream through rocks and mud another 1/10 mile to a launching spot. The water level fluctuates drastically as the dam opens and closes, and water can wash down the river below in a mini-tidal wave inches high when the dam is

opened. We were once cooling off after the carry with a swim when one such wave suddenly descended and thoroughly soaked our clothes which we had folded neatly on a flat rock beside the water. The canoe was afloat by the time we salvaged our clothes; fortunately, following our usual custom, we had tied it securely. The water level quickly rose another 2 feet.

The water along this stretch runs fast, with riffles and some turbulence. The Passumpsic River (Mi. 1½) joins the Connecticut 1½ miles below the dam. Paddle an easy half mile up the Passumpsic to see a pretty gorge just below the last dam on that river. An easy rapid lies by the river mouth and riffles continue below it. According to local fishermen, the deep pools interspersed among these riffles hide lunkers. Below, the river flows more quickly around some small islands.

Land on the left above the Monroe bridge to portage the McIndoe Falls Dam just below (Mi. 6¾). The bank here is steep and muddy. Carry less than ¼ mile across the paved road and down a dirt track to a sandy cove. McIndoe Falls Dam gives fishermen and canoeists below a sporting chance by sounding a horn when the gates are opened.

McIndoe Falls to Woodsville *(8¼ miles).*
Fast water continues 4 miles to the dam at East Ryegate (Mi. 10¾). A conspicuously sharp bend to the left precedes the dam, and a factory rises from the right bank just below the dam. You have the unpleasant choice here of washing over the dam or wading through poison ivy. Land on the left. The higher the water the longer the carry through the poison ivy. The footing is poor through mud and over rough ledges. Access here is downsteam of the dam and factory on the Vermont side.

Below the dam, the river widens and has some shallow spots. After 3 miles you reach Woodsville Narrows (Mi. 13¾), notable for its sharp S-curves and narrow passes through high cliffs. Rapids run the length of the narrows; beyond them, whirlpools create some turbulence in the broad pool just above the mouth of the Ammonoosuc River. Wells River enters a short distance downstream just below the Woodsville bridge (Mi. 15).

Woodsville was once the head of navigation on the Connecticut, with canals and locks circumventing dams and rapids downstream. Early commercial vessels were flatboats which were sailed up the river when there was enough wind and poled up when there was not. After steamboats were introduced to the river, attempts to venture further upstream to Barnet, Vermont (above McIndoe Falls) followed, and the *Barnet* was built specifically for the run. Unfortunately, her designers neglected to check the dimensions of the locks around the Bellows Falls rapids; the *Barnet* didn't fit and was

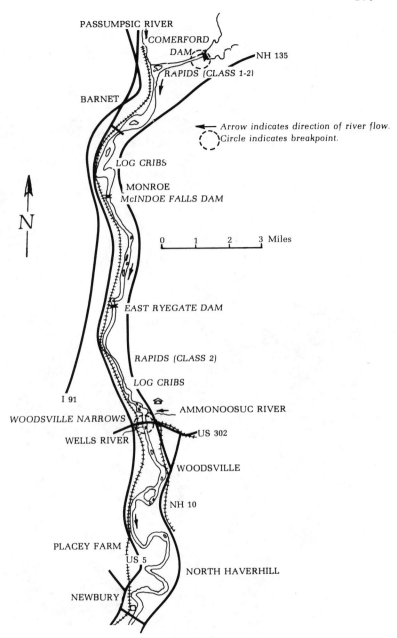

Connecticut River - part 4

Picking wild grapes from the canoe.

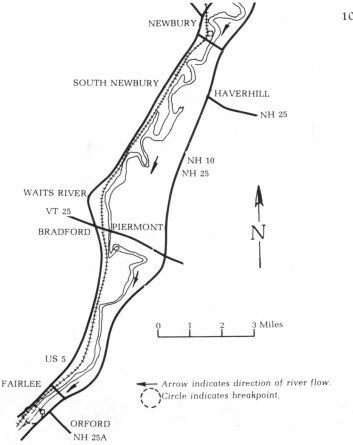

NEWBURY

SOUTH NEWBURY

HAVERHILL

NH 25

NH 10
N'H 25

WAITS RIVER

VT 25

BRADFORD   PIERMONT

N

0   1   2   3 Miles

US 5

FAIRLEE

← Arrow indicates direction of river flow.
⟨ ⟩ Circle indicates breakpoint.

ORFORD
NH 25A

Connecticut River - part 5

forced to retire downstream in ignominy. The advent of railroads ended commercial navigation on the Connecticut.

Woodsville to Newbury *(10½ miles)*.

Fast riffles continue below the high Woodsville bridge for ½ mile. Smooth water with a fair current and some shallow spots in low water follows as the river winds to Newbury. The Placey Farm (Mi. 18), its name conspicuous in large white letters on a red barn, marks the beginning of backwater from Wilder Dam 45 miles south. The river gradually becomes slower and deeper, although the valley is so steep that the lake formed by the dam is not noticeable. A launching ramp on the right upstream of the Newbury bridge (Mi. 25½) offers a possible take-out.

Newbury to Orford *(18 miles).*

Further downstream, the covered bridge connecting South Newbury to Haverhill collapsed just after it had been refurbished and made into a state park. Access is possible but not particularly good from the New Hampshire side. The river continues its slow and circuitous course past the Waits River mouth (Mi. 34¾) and the Bradford bridge (Mi. 36) to Orford (Mi. 43). You may take out on the left at the launching ramp (Mi. 43½) ½ mile below the Orford bridge or continue downstream to the many campgrounds, picnic areas, or launching ramps along the 20-mile stretch to Wilder Dam.

Placey Farm

14 White River— Connecticut River

Miles	Cumulative Miles	Break Points	River Rating	Special Difficulties
	0	**White River** Granville		
7¼			1	
	7¼	Lions Park		
9½			Q,1,2	
	16¾	Stockbridge		
9			2	
	25¾	Bethel		
11¾			Q,1	Occasional ledges (class 2)
	37½	Sharon		
6¼			2	Old dam
	43¾	West Hartford		
4½			Q,1	Ledge
	51	**Connecticut River**		
7¾			Q,1	Falls*
	58¾	Sumner Falls		

*Does not require portage if taking out at break point.

The White River, in combination with the Winooski and its tributary the Mad River, was a main Indian route between lower New England and Montreal. However, it was the easy travel through the valley to the lower mountain passes rather than the river itself which made this a well-traveled route. The White is a rocky river with a quick current, and along its upper reaches can only be run during high or medium water. Although it is not extremely difficult and is popular with canoeing groups, the White is the most demanding river described in this guidebook.

The upper river is best run in May when the water level is high or after a heavy rain. The river below Bethel can be run in a moderately wet summer but not in very dry weather. Its clear water and pools invite swimming, and its pleasantly fast current makes this a good river to use as practice for white water canoe camping trips. You get the feeling of handling a loaded boat in a current in the easy water at the start below the Lions Park while the rapids below Stockbridge require considerable maneuvering skill. Some of the riffles below Bethel require good water reading, and the ledges give a chance to run through high waves. Roads along the river offer refuge in case of an accident.

The White River rises in Skylight Pond, a beautiful little spot which can be reached by a 5-mile hike north on the Long Trail from VT 125

Dragging canoe over a shallow, rocky rapid.

White River - part 1

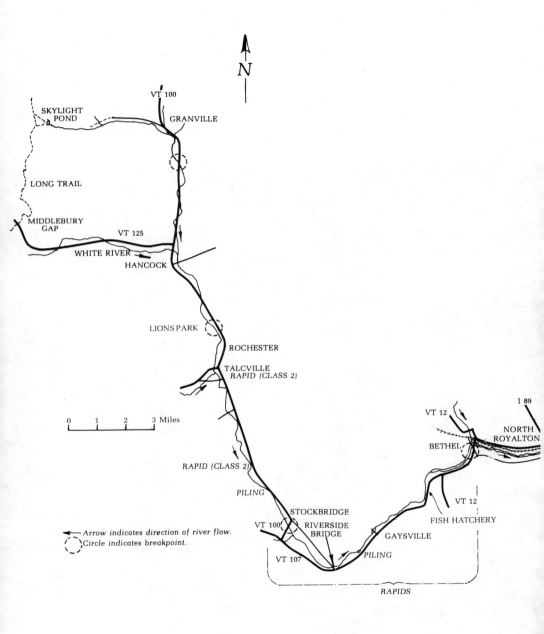

in Middlebury Gap. Once my daugther and I followed the river from
Skylight Pond, where it leaves as a tiny trickle, to its confluence with
the Connecticut at White River Junction. For its first 2 miles, it
splashes over rocks and under moss down the side of the mountain.
A drivable dirt road follows it down the next 3 miles to Granville,
where it becomes navigable near the first VT 100 bridge.

   From this point, the river offers 51 miles of almost unobstructed
canoeing to the Connecticut at White River Junction, with another
7¾ unimpeded miles down the Connecticut to Sumner Falls. This is
the longest almost continuously rapid run without a carry in the area.

Shallow riffles challenge your water reading skill.

Fishing from a home made kayak.

WHITE RIVER

Granville to Lions Park *(7¼ miles).*

This 7¼-mile stretch is runnable in high water only. Put in where VT 100 crosses the White just below Granville. Here the river is small with a fast current and is sometimes obstructed by fallen trees.

VT 100 crosses three times along this stretch. The river also passes beneath a side road bridge below Hancock (Mi. 4¼).

Lions Park to Stockbridge *(9½ miles).*

Lions Park (Mi. 7¼), on the left bank about 1 mile above Rochester on VT 100, is the usual put-in for a run down the upper portion of the White. The VT 73 bridge crosses 1½ miles from the park, and ½ mile below, the West Branch entering from the right almost doubles the river's size.

A class 2 rapid runs above and below the Talcville bridge (Mi. 9½) and is easily seen from the bridge and from VT 100. The river then curves in leisurely fashion through a cow pasture where it scatters around several sandy islands.

After 3 miles of easy going, the river turns right and divides around another island. Land on the left bank beside the island to scout a class 2 rapid (Mi. 12¾) which lies beneath a high bank where the two channels rejoin and the river bends to the left. Below the rapid, the river again flows easily as far as Stockbridge (Mi. 16¾).

Stockbridge to Bethel (9 miles).
One of the more difficult stretches of rapids runs from Stockbridge to Gaysville. These rapids run class 2 in medium water and up to class 3 in high water with eddies and considerable waves. In places the river is wide, and in medium water the current sifts evenly among the rocks, challenging your water-reading skills. You cannot run this stretch in low water.

Waves on the outside corner under the Riverside bridge (Mi. 19½), 2¾ miles below Stockbridge, can swamp or upset a canoe. One mile further downstream, an old bridge piling lies in the middle of the river (Mi. 20½); it can be run on the right or on the left, but not through the middle, although indecisive canoeists occasionally try.

Where VT 107 climbs high on the right and the river swings left, the water drops through some big rocks with high standing waves. A pool lies below and a picnic area sits high up the bank on the right. Beyond the pool and around the corner, the river passes over an awkward ledge which you can scout in advance from the picnic area. This rapid has changed considerably during the past 20 years, as the river rearranges the rocks with each storm.

As the river approaches the high cliff at Gaysville, it swings left through another fast outside corner with standing waves. A privately owned campground fronts the river's right bank just below the bridge in Gaysville.

Beyond Gaysville the rapids become less continuous, although two steep ledges about ½ mile apart not far from Gaysville and clearly visible from VT 107 still require attention. A fish hatchery lies on the right just west of the junction of VT 107 and VT 12.

As the valley widens, the river also becomes wider and fans out over a series of gravel bars. The Third Branch enters from the left just above the VT 107-12 bridge at Bethel. An excellent access lies on the right upstream of the bridge (Mi. 25¾).

Bethel to Sharon (11¾ miles).
The river below Bethel can be run in a fairly wet summer, but in

Bow paddler reaches out to draw canoe to right; stern paddler prys stern to right to move canoe directly sideways.

After a good night's sleep.

drier weather the riffles over the gravel bars require some wading.
On a warm day this is not at all unpleasant.

Wherever the White makes a sharp left turn the rock configuration
causes the water to be deeper, faster, and rougher on the outside
(right side) of the curve. Therefore, in low water you should keep to
the right for the deeper channels, and in high water keep to the left
for channels not runnable in lower water. Where the river curves to
the right, no particular patterns prevail.

To begin a trip at Bethel, put in on the right above the VT 107-12
bridge. One mile from the Bethel bridge a fast drop lies immediately
below the site of an old power dam (Mi. 26¾).

From here the 10-mile run to Sharon is generally easy in medium
water, with frequent riffles and occasional class 1 to 2 ledges. Just
below the high I-89 bridge (Mi. 28½), a side road on the left comes
close and offers access to the river. The Second Branch enters from
the left just above the North Royalton bridge (Mi. 29½), and in
another 1¾ miles you reach the small town of Royalton (Mi. 31¼).
One-half mile further downstream, a railroad bridge crosses the river

over a small island. About 1 mile below the island, a large rock ledge just out from the left shore just below a transverse ledge. Most people look this ledge over before running it. This big rocky ledge with its huge pool below makes a delightful spot to land for a picnic and swim.

This ledge and all other difficult spots from here down to Hartford, except for an old dam below Sharon, can be easily scouted in advance from VT 14. However, a strong class 2 party may not need to look these over again before running them.

The First Branch drains into the White River at South Royalton (Mi. 33), which is in fact northeast of Royalton. The ledge just below the bridge here is best scouted in advance from the bridge. Another mile brings you to a small group of sandy islands whose shorelines change with each storm.

Just above Sharon, I-89 recrosses the river (Mi. 36¾). The best take-out here is by a Quonset hut on the left bank between I-89 and the Sharon bridge (Mi. 37½).

Bowline know affixes painter to canoe; two half hitches on a bight secure the painter to the post.

White River - Connecticut River

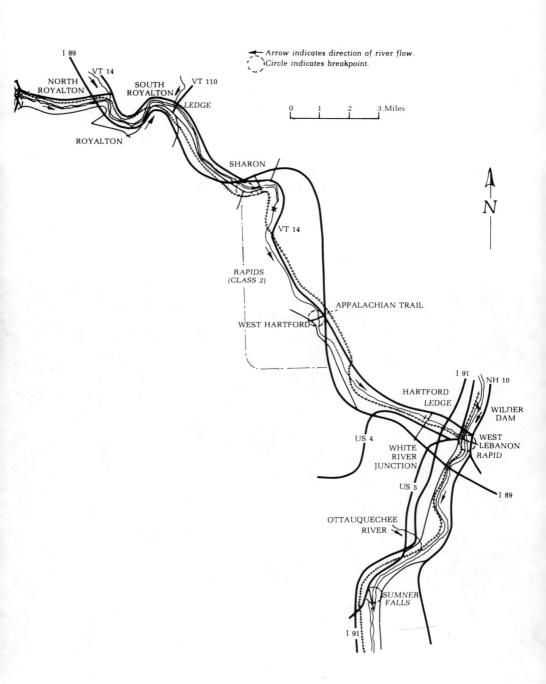

Sharon to West Hartford *(6¼ miles).*

From Sharon to West Hartford, ledges similar to those already passed occur with greater frequency. The most difficult spot from Bethel to Hartford lies 1¾ miles below the Sharon bridge where the river swings right and VT 14 climbs high on the left. High abutments on each bank indicate where an old dam lies at the foot of the mountain notch here (Mi. 39¼). In medium water the dam is best run on the right or lined or carried on the left. The backroller is strong enough to trap a canoe. Although this dam is difficult to scout in advance, a dirt track off VT 14 at the southern end of the mountain does lead

Swamping below the old dam at Sharon.

partway to the dam. The river and the road meet again near a railroad bridge ½ mile below; put in here if you wish to avoid the dam.

The ledges over the next 4 miles to West Hartford provide an enjoyable class 2 run at medium water, with drops and high waves alternating with smoother sections. Many places have a fair current and waves, but no rocks and a good run-out, and offer excellent opportunities to practice canoe rescues and swimming in rapids.

The large island ½ mile above West Hartford (Mi. 43¾) has a 3-foot ledge on the left which requires a fair amount of water to run. The drop on the right where the river breaks into three channels around a sweeping curve, is more gradual.

West Hartford to Connecticut River *(4¼ miles).*
The West Hartford bridge (Mi. 43¾), crossed by the Appalachian Trail, marks the end of the White's most exciting rapids and many canoe groups take out here.

The remaining 7¼ miles to the Connecticut, however, do contain some riffles and ledges and offer a good quickwater run. A fast current brings you to a big ledge just above the Hartford bridge (Mi. 49½) where another possible take-out is upstream on the right bank. It is another 1½ miles through the city of White River Junction and under several bridges to the Connecticut River (Mi. 51).

CONNECTICUT RIVER

White River to Sumner Falls *(7¾ miles).*

The run on the Connecticut River to the take-out above Sumner Falls (also called the Hartland Rapid) offers an additional 7¾ miles with only two short runnable drops which kick up some waves. However, water levels can fluctuate wildly and suddenly along this stretch; this depends on the power requirements of the Wilder Dam electrical generating plant, 2 miles north of White River Junction. (A Visitor's Information Center is at the New Hampshire end of the dam.)

The I-89 bridge crosses high overhead 1¼ miles below the confluence, and ½ mile beyond, a small island marks the first easy drop. Another 3 miles of paddling bring you to the mouth of the Ottauquechee River (Mi. 56¼) on the right, and shortly after to more high waves at the second drop.

Watch for a large rock in the middle of the river 2 miles below the second drop. This rock, which poses no problem itself, signals that you are approaching the dangerous Sumner Falls. A warning sign is sometimes posted on the Vermont side. After a sweeping curve to the left, rocky ledges appear on the right shore and in the middle of the river.

Take out on the right above the rock outcropping (Mi. 58¾) where a sign should mark the portage. Although the first rapids look trivial, each successive drop gets worse, culminating in a series of falls which lie out of view beyond the far island.

In high water the river thunders impressively over the falls, while in low water the bared ledges reveal a series of interestingly scoured potholes. If you walk out to inspect the potholes, be extremely careful as the ledges are worn smooth and coated with silt and mud. Remember also that a head of water released from Wilder Dam can sweep down the river without warning. You can easily launch a canoe below the falls for sightseeing.

The recommended take-out above the north outcropping leads to a picnic area with fireplaces; you can reach this by car by following a dirt road east off US 5. This road is about 3.2 miles south of the Ottauquechee River bridge and just north of an I-89 underpass.

Guidebooks from The Countryman Press and Backcountry Publications

Written for people of all ages and experience, these popular and carefully prepared books feature detailed trail and tour directions, notes on points of interest and natural phenomena, maps and photographs.

Walks and Rambles Series

Walks and Rambles on the Delmarva Peninsula, $9.95
Walks and Rambles in Dutchess and Putnam Counties (NY), $9.95
Walks and Rambles in Rhode Island, $9.95
Walks and Rambles in the Upper Connecticut River Valley, $9.95
Walks and Rambles in Westchester (NY) and Fairfield (CT) Counties, $8.95

Biking Series

25 Mountain Bike Tours in Vermont, $9.95
25 Bicycle Tours on Delmarva, $8.95
25 Bicycle Tours in Eastern Pennsylvania, $8.95
20 Bicycle Tours in the Finger Lakes, $8.95
20 Bicycle Tours in the 5 Boroughs (NYC), $8.95
25 Bicycle Tours in the Hudson Valley, $9.95
25 Bicycle Tours in Maine, $9.95
25 Bicycle Tours in New Hampshire, $7.95
25 Bicycle Tours in New Jersey, $8.95
20 Bicycle Tours in and around New York City, $7.95
25 Bicycle Tours in Vermont, $8.95

Canoeing Series

Canoe Camping Vermont and New Hampshire Rivers, $7.95
Canoeing Central New York, $10.95
Canoeing Massachusetts, Rhode Island and Connecticut, $7.95

Hiking Series

50 Hikes in the Adirondacks, $11.95
50 Hikes in Central New York, $9.95
50 Hikes in Central Pennsylvania, $9.95
50 Hikes in Eastern Pennsylvania, $10.95
50 Hikes in the Hudson Valley, $10.95
50 Hikes in Massachusetts, $11.95
50 More Hikes in New Hampshire, $9.95
50 Hikes in New Jersey, $10.95
50 Hikes in Northern Maine, $10.95
50 Hikes in Ohio, $12.95
50 Hikes in Southern Maine, $10.95
50 Hikes in Vermont, $11.95
50 Hikes in West Virginia, $9.95
50 Hikes in Western New York, $12.95
50 Hikes in Western Pennsylvania, $11.95
50 Hikes in the White Mountains, $12.95

Adirondack Series

Discover the Adirondack High Peaks, $14.95
Discover the Central Adirondacks, $8.95
Discover the Eastern Adirondacks, $9.95
Discover the Northeastern Adirondacks, $9.95
Discover the Northern Adirondacks, $10.95
Discover the Northwestern Adirondacks, $12.95
Discover the South Central Adirondacks, $10.95
Discover the Southeastern Adirondacks, $9.95
Discover the Southern Adirondacks, $10.95
Discover the Southwestern Adirondacks, $9.95
Discover the West Central Adirondacks, $13.95

Ski-Touring Series

25 Ski Tours in Central New York, $8.95
25 Ski Tours in New Hampshire, $8.95
25 Ski Tours in Vermont, $8.95

Other Guides

Maine: An Explorer's Guide, $14.95
New England's Special Places, $12.95
New Jersey's Special Places, $12.95
New York State's Special Places, $12.95
Pennsylvania Trout Streams and their Hatches, $14.95
Vermont: An Explorer's Guide, $16.95
Waterfalls of the White Mountains, $14.95

The above titles are available at bookstores and at certain sporting goods stores or may be ordered directly from the publisher. For complete descriptions of these and other guides, write: The Countryman Press, P.O. Box 175, Woodstock, VT 05091.